by the same author

The Crêpe and Pancake Cookbook
Freezer to Microwave Cookery
The Colour Book of Microwave Cooking
Microwave Cooking
Microwave Cookery for the Housewife
The Heartwatcher's Cookbook

The Sociable Slimmer

The Sociable Slimmer's Cookbook

Cecilia Norman

Illustrated by Kate Simunek
Photographs by Roger Tuff

Hutchinson

London Melbourne Sydney Auckland Johannesburg

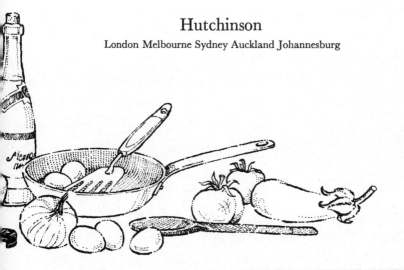

Hutchinson & Co. (Publishers) Ltd

An imprint of the Hutchinson Publishing Group

3 Fitzroy Square, London W1P 6JD

Hutchinson Group (Australia) Pty Ltd
30–32 Cremorne Street, Richmond South, Victoria 3121
PO Box 151, Broadway, New South Wales 2007

Hutchinson Group (NZ) Ltd
32–34 View Road, PO Box 40–086, Glenfield, Auckland 10

Hutchinson Group (SA) Pty Ltd
PO Box 337, Bergvlei 2012, South Africa

First published 1981
© Cecilia Norman 1981

Illustrations © Hutchinson Publishing Group Ltd 1981

Set in Monotype Baskerville

Printed in Great Britain by The Anchor Press Ltd
and bound by Wm Brendon & Son Ltd
both of Tiptree, Essex

ISBN 0 09 143110 7

Contents

Colour pictures
between pages 80 and 81; 176 and 177

Preface

The idea for this book was born out of the problems of my fluctuatingly fat, married daughter, Dilys, who regularly entertains; she is also an enthusiastic eater and thus the perfect guest. She has tried every known slimming method, bar surgery, and has finally managed to nail the problem. The system is one of removing guilty feelings by permitting over-indulgence on certain occasions in a calorie-controlled diet.

I have included as many tips as I can to alert you to the warning signs of high-calorie foods, but the last thing I want to do is 'preach'. We slimmers, like alcoholics, have to reach our own psychological rock bottom before taking ourselves in hand and embarking on a reducing programme. If you can succeed just once, you will be confident that you can summon up the will-power to do it again. Some worthy people manage to slim and stay that way. They are not always the happiest of people, for what pleasure can there be in a lifetime of self-denial? The majority diet spasmodically and, if you can regain your goal weight whenever *you* decide, that is surely all that is needed.

This book is not intended to be a slimming manual, but to help those already slimming to continue to socialize without misery. Since I do not profess to have any medical knowledge, you should consult your doctor before embarking on any slimming régime.

So my thanks to Dilys and also my patient guinea pigs, Kerry and Colin Lambert and Thomas Tausz, to my husband Laurie who is my indispensable backroom boy, and Jenny Wigley who prepared the food for the photography and to Roger Tuff for the photographs. Thanks also to the General Trading Company Ltd of Sloane Street, London, for the loan of the table lamp in the dinner party photograph and various dishes and glasses in the other photographs including the tureen for the *moules marinière*, ramekins, lotus bowls and Regency goblets.

Introduction

The Slimming Problem in General

'Slimming' must be one of the most overworked words in our vocabulary, and when we talk of weight reduction we do not always discuss ourselves but refer to 'figures' in general and wonder why our fat friend doesn't slim. Our fat friend does *try* to slim, but unless you are a fattie you cannot comprehend how difficult it is.

Slimming talk is very boring, but crash diets, low-carbohydrate diets, low-fat diets, high-protein diets, banana or grapefruit diets, and the Mayo Clinic, form the basis for endless argument. Non-slimmers find this unbearable, so please confine your remarks to your own sort. Go to a slimming club, preferably taking a fatter friend with you (to make you feel thin), and there you will find the conversation scintillating.

Slimming clubs, which are very good, fall into two types. The most well known is Weightwatchers, where you follow a set diet, eating certain things at certain times of the day; the other clubs rely on strict calorie control, often tailoring the diet to suit the client. In both, you are weighed communally at each visit and, as you have to pay whether you go or not, you are likely to attend regularly in order to get your money's worth.

If you are tremendously overweight or in the waddling category, you have no choice but to attend one of these clubs. There is often a rapid weight loss at the beginning of the course, giving you the impetus to carry on. Stick it out for six months and you will discover a new 'you'. However, a natural fattie will never turn into a thinnie without a lifetime of misery, so you may prefer to diet for three months and eat for nine.

Slimming clubs are helpful psychologically and the mind plays a very large part whichever way you choose to diet. No one can slim for you; even the vibrating rubber pads wired up to the electric current can only consolidate what you've got.

You should carry out a little self-analysis before starting to diet. Why do you want to slim? Is it for health reasons? The horror on your man's face as he surveys the mountains of flesh when you undress? Or are you yearning for a particularly pretty size 12 dress in the high street window?

Look at the weight charts on page 227 to get some idea of what your ideal weight should be. You can quite easily calculate how many daily calories you need. The body uses up calories even when completely immobile. During sleep 1 calorie for each $2\frac{1}{4}$ pounds (1 kilogram) of body weight is lost per hour. An 8 stone 9 pound (55 kilogram) person burns up 440 calories in an eight-hour night. Brisk exercise uses up the greatest number of calories, but, because it is difficult to maintain this for any length of time, gentle physical activity may be more effective. A half-hour walk at dog-walking speed will work off 170 calories, jogging will benefit you by 240 calories for the same length of time. Planned exercise may not work because, if you were already interested in your fitness, you would not have the bulges you can see now. However, you could resolve to walk to the next bus stop – it is surprising how quickly one gets used to this.

There is a simple calculation to ascertain how many calories you need for maintaining even weight. Multiply your weight in pounds by ten and add half as much again. So our 8 stone 9 pound friend needs 121 multiplied by ten = 1210 plus 605 = 1815 calories. If the same person lay absolutely still in bed all day, she would still require at least 1350 calories. Any exercise or energy expended will make her lighter, and any food or drink consumed the converse. To maintain constant weight the energy books must balance. To lose weight make sure your energy expenditure is in credit. If you are considerably overweight, you are probably hungrier than the thinnie. A drastic diet will be very difficult to keep up, so don't try to eat less than 1500 calories a day. The 20 stoner expends much more energy than the person who is only slightly overweight, because of the increased effort required to move about – think how much more fatigued you are after a morning's gardening pushing a loaded wheelbarrow.

You have to lose 3500 calories in order to work off 1 pound of body fat. If your excess is only a few pounds, you have to reduce your intake to 1000 calories a day to achieve a weekly weight loss of 2 pounds. It is surprising how little you have to forego to cut out 100 calories at a stroke, as the chart on page 21 demonstrates.

You will soon learn to add up calories and recognize food by its fattening capacity rather than its appearance. Always calculate on the high side, putting the count up to the next 10.

When you cut down on carbohydrates, there is a dramatic initial weight loss, but this is misleading because it will be fluid only that you are losing – notice how many more times you need to visit the toilet – but it does give the impetus to start the diet. The danger of a regular low-carbohydrate diet is that you might over-compensate with fats and protein foods, thus defeating the purpose of the exercise. Follow a low-carbohydrate diet for a few days, then after the first week start on a calorie-controlled plan.

Initially diet for five days a week. Weekend slimming not only makes you a bore to live with but also to entertain. Work out your daily calorie allowance, taking into account the inevitable splurge on Saturday and Sunday. Strictness is possible only because you have something to look forward to, but even so you will have to watch it just a little at the weekends. You may prefer to go berserk one evening a week, but never tell yourself you won't bother to diet today. Tomorrow you will feel guilty and be a real old misery.

Stomachs can play some dirty tricks and their owners must always be alert. Fatties by nature can make themselves even larger by nibbling at home. You may tell yourself that you have to taste the cooking and your tummy will encourage you. To defeat this, set aside one day a week only for cooking, and store or freeze the week's meals; then you will nibble on that day only. It requires but a short time to thaw and reheat these dishes, and a microwave oven is a boon for this. Unfortunately, the more you eat the hungrier you feel, and this hunger is often accompanied by a feeling of nausea.

Mothers have a particular problem. Young children invariably leave bits and pieces of their food, which have probably been chosen in the first place for quality. It seems such a waste, so Mum automatically picks them up between finger and thumb to swallow in the unguarded moment. Say to yourself, 'I'm not a dustbin.' School children, coming home ravenous, expect a good tea or they will raid the larder. Cook them the food you really dislike and then you won't be tempted to fit in an extra meal.

If you have to spend a lot of time in the kitchen, prepare some low-calorie nibbles: a wadge of lettuce, a few raw mushrooms or perhaps a carrot. You will find a more comprehensive list on page 228. You must discover what helps you slim the most. It could be coffee, which has a diuretic effect, as well as being a stimulant, or tea, or canned low-calorie fizzy drinks. Home-made chicken soup is a good standby, pleasantly warming in cold weather, but remember not to eat bread with it. A few tiny pieces of broken spaghetti can be popped in to make it more like a meal. It is better to make soup almost too hot to drink, and blowing on each spoonful makes it last longer and so seem a bigger meal.

Diet discipline is best attained by portion control. Let others do the work for you. It might cost more but it is well worth investing in pre-wrapped butter pats and cheese portions. Camembert is now available in 1 oz rather than $1\frac{5}{8}$ oz segments and processed cheese is packed in ready-to-use slices. Even jam can be purchased in individual foil containers, which are usually sold at the Cash and Carry, but your friendly neighbourhood grocer would order a carton for you. It is also better to use cube sugar than a teaspoon of sugar in drinks, but in the recipes I have given the amount in teaspoons. You should substitute liquid sweetener if you can. Slimming breads are not very satisfactory, and in any case you don't want to become a freak, living solely on diet foods. Eat wrapped, thin-cut bread which weighs 1 oz rather than 1½ oz per slice and, if you can't resist the smell of fresh master baker's bread avoid walking past his shop.

You will be amazed how you can brainwash yourself into detesting foods you previously loved. Who likes sausage rolls anyway, I ask myself. Never buy high-calorie foods or even irresistible low-calorie items that you are going to scoff limitlessly. The family can do without cream and those delicious crumbly English cheeses; if you finally succumb to cheese, grate it finely and it will go much further. Should you prefer to weigh out your cheese ration and you slightly exceed the intended amount, watch that you don't eat that little left-over piece and always buy the smallest eggs, apples, oranges and other things that are sold individually. When cooking a 'whole' item, such as a joint of meat, cut your own slices wafer thin.

When you are going out for the day, take an apple with you, well wrapped in a plastic bag so that it doesn't fill the air with its aroma. Then if, and only if, no other food turns up, the apple will take the edge off your appetite, but you are not allowed to have it in addition to a lunchtime coffee-bar snack. Stay out of the house at mealtimes whenever possible, as hunger will die away as the hour passes. One of the finest slimming aids I know is to cut out supper alto-gether and go to bed – not an easy thing to do when others are dependent on you for sustenance and/or company.

It is an inescapable fact of life that you have the frame and figure that your parents gave you. Some people have large bosoms and small hips, while others are flat up top with heavy behinds. Exercise will firm the flab, and diet will lessen the load, but it may not be in your required area. Although the male is differently built, the problem is the same for him, so be realistic and don't hope for miraculous reshaping. Use a skirt or trousers instead of scales to check yourself, for like the mirror a waistband doesn't lie and, if the top button will not do up, you are too fat. Always weigh on the same scales, preferably at home undressed, in private, and at the same time each week. More frequent checks are supposed to be a waste of time, but I make them just the same.

This book isn't meant to dictate how you should slim, but rather to provide recipes and meal suggestions within your calorie-controlled structure. Slimming is not any fun at all and the advice in this chapter has been gathered from personal, painful experience. I hope it may be of some help.

The Sociable Slimmer's Dilemma

How to reduce without becoming a recluse is a perennial problem. The plight of the would-be slimmer when faced with a busy social life is filled with contradictions. On the one hand you want to adhere to a diet, and on the other you wish to 'eat, drink and be merry'. If you entertain frequently, you will have come up against the problem of providing dishes which are attractive and at the same time low in calories. Only a small proportion of your guests is likely to be on a slimming diet, and people who need to be careful with diet realize that they will have to do the best they can when invited out to eat; if they are not prepared to compromise, they should not accept the invitation in the first place.

The dieting hostess can help in many ways. There is no real need to load dishes with butter, cream and alcohol. In most instances the fat content can be reduced and cream can be offered separately. Alcohol should be used sparingly, unless the dish is to be flambéed, when the alcohol will evaporate. Cut down on the sugar – indeed not everyone has a sweet tooth. Give a choice of wine including one which will be lower in calories. Don't press second helpings on to the guests – this places them in an invidious position – and whenever possible allow them to help themselves.

To economize on fat, use non-stick pans for cooking, grill rather than fry, and bake or roast as dry as possible with the minimum added fat. Vegetables, salads and fruit are mainly low-calorie items, and it is possible to produce a wide selection of starters using them. One could start with plain fruit juices though this is rather boring. The judicial use of bottled low-calorie dressings, low-fat soft cheese and yogurt can be undetectable, and, where butter or butter sauces are habitually served, offer them separately. The hostess' portion of main courses can be reduced, but this should not bother your guests, and slimmers amongst them can always ask for a small portion. Choose the less fatty cuts of meat and don't overload the main course by serving pastry, pudding or mashed potato crusts; modify ordinary recipes – Yorkshire pudding, for example, can be made with nearly all water instead of all milk. Serve at least one plainly cooked vegetable, and there is no harm in offering as many as four different vegetables, including potatoes or rice. It is surprising how we kid ourselves that we don't eat potatoes and then take just one or two. A plain side salad never comes amiss, for then the grateful dieter guest can be seen to be eating heartily. Serve a choice of two desserts from the recipe section and one other fattening sweet, such as a pie, steamed pudding or crème brulée. The hostess and dieter guests then will not spoil the pleasure of the others.

I always prepare a cheese board, garnished with celery, tomato halves and radishes, and include lower calorie cheeses, such as Edam, Austrian smoked and Brie, as well as the extravagant Gorgonzola and Stilton. If you are only going to eat a small piece of cheese yourself, there won't be a vast calorie difference between any of the cheeses. Serve cream separately with the coffee and offer a chocolate mint to round off the dinner.

The dieter guest has different problems. To call attention to the fact that you are dieting is a great mistake. Other people may then taunt you and gleefully force extras on you and you will be sorry you ever spoke. Keep it a secret and you need not upset your diet unduly. It may also be considered rude if you refuse all the delicacies that are heaped on your plate. Everyone eats out from time to time and it is perfectly possible to be the ideal guest even while slimming. No one on a rigid weight-reducing régime can happily eat in company if all his or her diet allows is half a grapefruit and a few raw vegetables washed down with un-limited black coffee. Slimmers must have a balanced diet and one meal a day won't do. Calorie control is the best and the longest lasting method. It is by this means that socializing becomes possible. You will soon learn how to recognize the more fattening foods. No one will mind if you refuse the roll and butter or the unfairly dreaded potato. Ask for water as well as wine and then you can have a glass of each, thus saving a few more calories. Water is best to quench your thirst, so don't waste calories on wine for that purpose. At parties you can drink water in a small glass and everyone will think you are drinking vodka. If your hostess gives you a choice, you can have the least fattening dish and, although it is impolite to leave meat on your plate, you don't have to mop up all the sauce, and don't add salt, which will make you thirsty. If, in addition, you refuse obvious extras like cream and the liqueur, you should be able to restrict your calorie intake to the mini-mum. A selected dinner out could be as little as 1000 calories, rising to 3500 on a splurge, but no matter, you can put it right in a couple of days, using the compensatory recipes and suggestions in Part Two.

Although most of the recipes in Part One are designed to serve four, there are exceptions where I feel that, in order to produce the dishes easily and economically, it is necessary to increase the quantities. The portion sizes are average to mean. Each recipe gives the calorific value of a single portion rounded up to the nearest 5. This will give you the *maximum* calorie count for a portion; the slimmer should take a smaller than average serving, thereby reducing the count still further. Of course there will be occasions when you are entertaining larger numbers, and you can then double up the quantities. (Remember, of course, that multiplication of quantity does not necessarily mean an equal increase in the cooking times – this depends entirely on what you are cooking.) Whenever possible use a non-stick pan and do not interchange the metric and

Imperial equivalents. Where exactness is crucial, metric weights are given in grams; where it is less important, the weights are given in kilograms or fractions of a kilogram – in such cases they may include peel, skin, bones, etc. All spoon measurements are level. A teaspoon is 5 millilitres and a tablespoon is 15 millilitres.

Though the term 'calorie' is often used very loosely, a calorie is in fact a definite measurement of energy: one calorie (strictly speaking a kilocalorie) is the amount of energy required to raise the temperature of 1 kg of water by 1°C. Calorific values of food are very difficult to measure exactly and I have taken an average from the many accepted sources I have consulted and rounded up the values where more convenient.

Very little will-power is required to cut down the daily calorie intake by 100 or 200. On the chart opposite, each item is about 100 calories; it is meant to be a guide only and not nutritional advice.

SAVE 100 CALORIES CHART

avocado	$\frac{1}{2}$
bacon	1 rasher
beer	$\frac{1}{2}$ pint
biscuits, semi-sweet	3
biscuits, sweet creams	2
bread, large sliced white	1 thick
bread, small sliced white	2 thick
bread roll	1
butter or margarine	1 walnut-sized piece
cheese, Cheddar	$2\frac{1}{2}$ cm x 3 cm (1 in. x $1\frac{1}{2}$ in.) cube
Gouda	5 cm (2 in.) cube
chocolate, plain or milk	3 squares
chocolates, filled	2
Cola-type drink	285 ml (10 fl. oz) can
cream, double	1 tablespoon without levelling
cream, single	2 tablespoons without levelling
eggs, boiled or poached	1 large
eggs, fried	$\frac{1}{2}$
figs, dried	2
fish finger, grilled	2
french dressing	2 tablespoons
ham	$\frac{3}{4}$ slice
mayonnaise	1 tablespoon
milk (whole)	1 teacup (150 ml, 5 fl. oz)
olive oil	2 teaspoons
potatoes, boiled	2 small
sausage, beef, grilled	1 large
sausage, pork, grilled	$\frac{1}{2}$ large
sausage roll	1 small
sherry	1 glass
spirits	1 double
sugar	5 lumps or 1 tablespoon without levelling
sweets, boiled	4

PART ONE

Recipes for the Entertaining Slimmer

I
Starters & Soups

AMERICAN GRAPEFRUIT

Slices of red-skinned apple form a fan spreading over the yellow fruit

The grapefruit are fiddly and time-consuming to prepare, but they look simply marvellous and make quite a conversation piece to start the dinner. Try to buy sweet-juice grapefruit – brown patches on the skin indicate sweetness. Test the weight in the palm of the hand and select the heaviest. The apples must be red-skinned for sweetness and contrasting colour.

Calories: **40** *(per half grapefruit)*

2 large grapefruit
1 red dessert apple
4 Maraschino cherries

Halve the grapefruit crosswise and loosen the segments with a grapefruit knife. Cut all the way round the outside edge to sever the membranes and slide the blade underneath the core to loosen it. Gently lift up the core and ease out the membrane. This should, with luck, come out in one. Notch the edges of the rind with scissors or a sharp knife. Quarter the apple, cut in half crosswise and remove the core. Cut thin slices and insert these, skin side up, between each of the grapefruit segments, pressing them well in to prevent discolouration. Top each grapefruit half with a cherry. *Serves 4.*

APPLE BASKETS

Raw, whole apple filled with celery, walnuts, cottage cheese and lemon juice – topped with a celery handle

We are always told to sprinkle cut apples with lemon juice to stop them darkening, but we are rarely given the reason for this happening. When an apple is cut the oxygen in the air causes browning, which in turn causes enzymes to start breaking down the apple's structure. The lemon juice contains a high quantity of acid, which is a preserving agent, so for complete freshness all the cut surfaces of an apple must be evenly covered.

Calories: 135

4 red dessert apples
1 to 2 tablespoons lemon
   juice
4 celery stalks

40 g (1½ oz) walnuts,
   chopped
100 g (4 oz) cottage cheese
½ celery stick for garnish

Wash and dry the apples and give them a good shine with a piece of kitchen paper sprinkled with the merest spot of vegetable oil. Cut off the tops and carefully remove the whole of the inside of the apples with a grapefruit knife, taking care not to break through the skins. Brush the inside walls with a little lemon juice. Remove the apple cores, chop the flesh and finely chop three of the celery stalks. Mix with the walnuts, cottage cheese and the remaining lemon juice and return mixture to apple skins. Cut the remaining celery stalk lengthwise into four. Plunge into boiling water for ½ minute. Drain and cool rapidly under cold running water and curve each piece to form a handle, pressing down into the apple baskets. *Serves 4.*

APPLE VICHYSSOISE

Hot apple, potato and leek soup with a swirl of soured cream

You must choose sharp cooking apples for this soup. Bramley's Seedlings, in season throughout the winter and spring, are my favourite because their flavour is so good. If you are lucky enough to have your own apple trees, pick the fruit when it is just ripe, and choose large apples, so that you won't have so much peeling and coring to do.

Calories: 125

1 medium onion, finely chopped
1 tablespoon vegetable oil
350 g (12 oz) cooking apples
175 g (6 oz) peeled potatoes
1 large leek, white part only, shredded finely
750 ml (1¼ pints) chicken stock
salt
white pepper
liquid sweetener (optional)
2 tablespoons soured cream
1 tablespoon freshly chopped parsley

Put the onion and oil in a large saucepan and cook gently until soft but not brown. Peel, core and chop the apples and chop the potatoes coarsely. Add to the pan with the leek, and stir continuously for a minute or two until all the vegetables are well mixed. Add the stock and bring to the boil, then reduce the heat as low as you can, cover and cook for about 20 minutes until the vegetables are soft. Liquidize or press the soup through a nylon sieve. Season to taste with salt and pepper, adding a few drops of liquid sweetener if you like. Reheat the soup, leaving it to simmer for a few minutes if it is too thin. Top each portion with soured cream and a sprinkling of parsley. *Serves 4.*

ASPARAGUS WITH SOURED CREAM

Asparagus simmered in chicken stock and coated in soured cream

Only fresh asparagus will do for a luxury dinner party. Canned asparagus is lovely but does not look as appetizing for a first course or starter.

Calories: 60

½ kg (1 lb) asparagus
300 ml (½ pint) well-
    flavoured chicken stock

6 tablespoons soured cream
salt
pepper

Remove all the tough ends from the asparagus and pare the stalks with a potato peeler. Tie the bunch with string a few inches up from the ends and stand it upright in a deep saucepan containing the hot stock. Cover with a lid or a dome made out of aluminium foil. Simmer gently until the stalks are cooked and the tips are sufficiently tender. Drain thoroughly, remove the string and arrange the asparagus in a large, shallow dish. Pour the cream over, liberally seasoned with salt and pepper. *Serves 4.*

AVOCADO, PRAWN AND GRAPEFRUIT COCKTAIL

Chopped avocado flesh, grapefruit and prawns in an unusual dressing – garnished with whole prawns

Avocado pears are a luxury fruit not normally included in a slimmer's menu because they are considered to be fattening. However, when teamed with low-calorie grapefruit and prawns, they go a very long way, so you will find that you are content with a smaller main course.

Calories: 165

1 tablespoon low-calorie
salad dressing
2 teaspoons white-wine
vinegar
½ teaspoon dry mustard
2 tablespoons natural, low-
fat yogurt

3 drops liquid sweetener
salt
pepper
2 medium avocados
1 large grapefruit
90 g (3½ oz) peeled prawns
4 whole prawns to garnish

In a large bowl beat the salad dressing, vinegar, sweetener, mustard and yogurt, and add salt and pepper to taste. Halve the avocados and scoop out the flesh, leaving the shells intact. Chop the flesh roughly. Segment and chop the grapefruit and toss lightly in the dressing with the avocado flesh and the peeled prawns. Pile back into the shells and garnish with the whole prawns. To keep the avocados' shape, preferably serve in avocado dishes, but they will look equally attractive embedded in a nest of crisply shredded lettuce. *Serves 4.*

BARBECUED SPARE RIBS

Traditional recipe using veal instead of pork

Use veal ribs instead of pork or lamb as veal has a lower calorie content. Spare ribs look as though they will make a substantial meaty meal but, fortunately for us slimmers, most of them is inedible bone, and you can go on chewing without adding any calories to your intake. Although meat is often grilled on a sheet of foil to help keep the pan clean, it is not a good idea because every drip of fat lost is a calorie saved. *Serve two ribs per person.*

Calories: 90

8 veal spare ribs
salt
pepper
2 tablespoons vinegar

2 tablespoons dry sherry
2 tablespoons tomato purée
2 tablespoons soy sauce
2 teaspoons clear honey

Separate the ribs, trim off excess fat and rub with salt and pepper. Combine the remaining ingredients, pour over the ribs and turn so that all sides are coated. Leave to marinate for at least 2 hours. Preheat the grill, arrange the ribs on the rack and cook for 5 minutes on each side. *Serves 4.*

CHICKEN AND EGG DROP SOUP

Thin chicken soup containing a nest of beaten egg strands

To keep the calorie count down, remove all the fat from stock before using. The easiest way to do this is to refrigerate or freeze as soon as stock is strained and cool. The fat will rise to the top during the cooling process and solidify in one easily removable disc. Chill in the narrowest possible jug and the job will be done in a jiffy.

Calories: 95

100 g (4 oz) cooked
   chicken
4 spring onions
1 l (2 pints) home-made
   chicken stock
½ teaspoon monosodium
   glutamate

salt
freshly ground white pepper
1 large egg, lightly beaten
1 tablespoon freshly
   chopped parsley

Shred the chicken and slice the onions thinly. Put them in a saucepan with the stock and monosodium glutamate, and add salt and pepper sparingly. Bring to the boil and simmer until reduced by about one-third. Taste and adjust the seasoning. While still very hot pour the mixture into a heated tureen. Give the egg a quick whisk with a fork and pour it into the soup through a strainer, moving the strainer's handle in a circular motion. Sprinkle with parsley. *Serves 4.*

CHICKEN STUFFED MUSHROOMS

Large, flat mushrooms topped with minced chicken and chives, lightened with egg white and baked in a slow oven

Not so many years ago button mushrooms were very expensive and the shops were full of the large, flat kind. All is now reversed; the small mushrooms are practically all 'factory-grown' and they don't stay in the soil long enough to grow big. If you find it difficult to buy the large, flat ones fresh, they are obtainable in cans.

Calories: 100

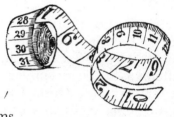

8 large, flat mushrooms
100 g (4 oz) cooked
  chicken, minced
1 large egg, separated
2 tablespoons chives,
  chopped

salt
pepper
25 g (1 oz) butter, melted
2 tablespoons soured cream

Cut off the mushroom stalks level with the caps, leaving part of the stalk – this will help keep the shape of the mushrooms when they are cooked. Arrange the caps, dark side up, in a greased, shallow dish. Mix the minced chicken with the egg yolk and the chives, and season with salt and pepper. Fold in the egg white, stiffly beaten, then heap a spoonful of the mixture on to each mushroom. Drizzle the melted butter over each cap. Cover the dish with foil and bake in a cool oven (150°C, 300°F, Gas 2) for ¾ hour. Lift the mushrooms out of the dish and gently place them on heated plates, pouring a little soured cream over the top of each for garnish and that little extra flavour. *Serves 4.*

DANISH CUCUMBER

Cucumber shells filled with a mixture of roll-mop herring, chopped egg and smoked salmon and garnished with fresh tarragon

The local delicatessen should stock most of the ingredients listed in this recipe but, if you find difficulty in obtaining some items, it can be made with various alternatives of your own choosing. I used tarragon which, among other fresh herbs, can often be purchased in ready-to-use packets – these herbs can be frozen without additional wrapping.

Fresh parsley can be substituted. Any variety of pickled herring can be used instead of the roll-mops, and smoked saithe, which comes in flat tins, can be substituted for the smoked salmon as it is very similar.

This starter may be garnished to give it a festive look. Stand the cucumber shells on a bed of shredded lettuce or red cabbage and put one or two lemon butterflies on each side as decoration if you wish.

Calories: 160

1 large cucumber
2 size 4 eggs, hard boiled
1 roll-mop herring
50 g (2 oz) smoked salmon
8 tablespoons soured cream

1 tablespoon fresh lemon
    juice
pepper
fresh tarragon sprigs

Top and tail the cucumber and cut into four. Immerse the pieces in a saucepan half-filled with boiling water. Bring back to the boil, then immediately remove the cucumber with a slotted spoon and plunge into cold water. Drain and dry. Halve each piece lengthwise and scoop out the pulp. Chop the drained pulp with the hard-boiled eggs, and cut the herring and salmon into strips. Mix them all lightly together in a bowl, then divide between the cucumber shells. Blend the cream with the lemon juice, and add pepper to taste. Spoon this over the cucumber and garnish with the tarragon. Serve two shells per person.   *Serves 4.*

CHILLED TOMATO SOUP

Tomato and cucumber soup perked up with Tabasco pepper sauce and fresh lemon juice

Many are the times that I have looked at a recipe and then made substitutions, particularly using canned instead of fresh tomatoes. But this recipe is specifically for a summer soup and the flavour really is different if you use fresh tomatoes rather than the canned variety. Please don't buy 'cooking' tomatoes, which have gone a bit soft or have the odd green, ·mouldy patch. They really cannot be trimmed up and retain a fresh flavour.

Calories: 60

½ kg (1 lb) firm, red tomatoes
1 large cucumber
300 ml (½ pint) canned tomato juice
2 tablespoons fresh lemon juice

salt
white pepper
few drops Tabasco pepper sauce
1 lemon, thinly sliced for garnish

Skin the tomatoes by immersing for a few minutes in boiling water, and peel the cucumber. Cut the tomato and cucumber flesh into small pieces and liquidize, or chop and pulp with a sharp knife. Press through a sieve into a large bowl and stir in the tomato and lemon juice. Add salt, pepper and Tabasco to taste. Pour mixture into a tureen and for garnish float slices of lemon on the top This recipe is best chilled for 4 to 6 hours before serving. *Serves 4.*

FRENCH ONION SOUP

Thick, dark, gooey soup full of onions

Traditionally French onion soup is served with a thin slice of toasted French bread glazed with cheese floating on the surface. This will add an extra 140 to 170 calories to each portion, so you may prefer to leave that for a main-course meal.

Calories: 110

½ kg (1 lb) onions
1 clove garlic
25 g (1 oz) butter
1½ l (3 pints) boiling water
5 tablespoons dry red wine

5½ oz can condensed
    consommé
salt
pepper
1 tablespoon grated
    Parmesan cheese

Peel and thinly slice the onions, crush the garlic and sauté onions and garlic together in the butter in a non-stick pan until just browning. Add all the other ingredients, but do not over-salt at this stage. Bring to the boil, then lower the heat to simmering; put on the lid just off centre, so that the steam can evaporate without the liquid boiling over. Cook and cook and cook until the soup is thick and gooey and reduced by half. Taste and adjust seasoning.   *Serves 4.*

HONOLULU COCKTAIL

A goblet of shredded lettuce topped with pineapple and prawns in a slightly curried sauce. Garnished with ground ginger and chopped red peppers

Dinner-party starters can serve two purposes. They titillate but they also take the edge off the appetite. I got the idea for this recipe and that for Melon Eliott (see below) from the Coed-y-Mwstwr Hotel in Coychurch, South Wales.

This is a hotel–restaurant that serves wonderful food, but much of it is certainly not for slimmers. Use cos lettuce as it takes up more space in the goblet. Wash the leaves, pat dry between paper towels, then pile the leaves one on top of the other and slice thinly with a sharp, stainless-steel knife. Wait until the last minute before filling the goblets, as the weight of the filling compresses the lettuce.

Calories: 80

2 tablespoons bottled low-calorie salad dressing
4 tablespoons natural low-fat yogurt
1 teaspoon curry powder
175 g (6 oz, 3 slices) fresh pineapple
75 g (3 oz) peeled prawns
heart of cos lettuce
¼ teaspoon ground ginger
2 teaspoons finely chopped raw red pepper

Combine the salad dressing, yogurt and curry powder. Chop the pineapple roughly and stir into the sauce with the prawns. Cover and refrigerate. About ½ hour before serving, shred the lettuce and half fill four large-stemmed glasses or goblets. Pile the prawn mixture on top, then sprinkle with ground ginger and the chopped red pepper. *Serves 4.*

MELON ELIOTT

Fresh melon balls and prawns in a tomato dressing set on a honeydew wedge – garnished with strips of smoked salmon

Melons come in all shapes and sizes. Strangely enough, the popular green- or yellow-skinned honeydew melon has double the calories of the canteloupe and ogen. However, since the honeydew is so much more readily available, I have used it in this recipe.

Calories: 110

4 wedges honeydew melon,
  seeds removed
50 g (2 oz) peeled prawns,
  halved
1 tablespoon low-calorie
  salad dressing

1 teaspoon fresh lemon
  juice
1 tablespoon tomato juice
25 g (1 oz) smoked salmon

Using a melon baller or teaspoon, loosen marble-sized balls from the melon flesh, leaving them resting on the skin. Sprinkle with the prawns. Blend the salad dressing, lemon juice and tomato juice together, drizzle the mixture over the melon, then garnish with thin strips of smoked salmon. *Serves 4.*

MELON WITH PARMA HAM

Wafer-thin slices of Parma ham draped over juicy melon wedges

What is ham? The hind leg or shoulder of pig, cured, smoked and generally cooked. Parma ham, amongst other continental varieties, is meant to be eaten as it comes. It has a clear and translucent colour. To prevent drying out, keep the ham well wrapped in waxed paper until just before serving.

Calories: 110

1 small honeydew melon
4 wafer-thin slices of
  Parma ham

4 thin-centre slices
  lemon

About 2 hours before dinner, cut the melon into four wedges. Remove the seeds and rind, leaving only the soft flesh. Put in the refrigerator or cold larder to chill. Just before serving, put on to individual plates and drape with a slice of ham. Top with a lemon ring. *Serves 4.*

MIDDLE EASTERN SOUP

A chilled soup of yogurt, lemon juice, herbs, prawns and cucumber

From freezer to table in 3 minutes if you have a liquidizer or food processor. Preparation time will be 10 to 15 minutes when carried out by hand. If frozen prawns are used without thawing, chilling will not be necessary. Otherwise chill for 2 hours before serving.

Calories: 105

600 ml (1 pint) natural, low-fat yogurt
1 teaspoon fresh lemon juice
2 mint leaves
4 sprigs parsley, stalks removed
4 chives

1 teaspoon sugar
50 g (2 oz) frozen peeled prawns
3 in. chunk of cucumber, cut into 4
freshly ground white pepper
salt
4 thin slices lemon

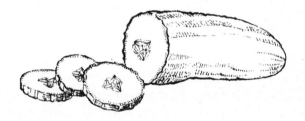

Put half the yogurt, the lemon juice, herbs and sugar in the liquidizer and blend for ½ minute. Add the prawns and cucumber and blend until chopped into small pieces but not puréed. Mix with the remaining yogurt and season to taste. Float a lemon slice in each individual bowl.   *Serves 4.*

MOULES MARINIÈRE

Stewed mussels in a gloriously flavoured thin soup

Moules Marinières is a mussel stew in which the mussels are eaten first; the liquid is then drunk as soup or mopped up with French bread (the latter is, of course, definitely not for the slimmer). An average serving is fifteen to twenty mussels. Count 10 Calories for each mussel. Inspect them before cooking and discard any that are even slightly open. Add salt only just before serving as mussels are quite salty in themselves.

Calories: 225

2 quarts mussels	squeeze lemon juice
1 onion, sliced	150 ml ($\frac{1}{4}$ pint) dry white
few sprigs parsley	wine
sprig thyme	1 teaspoon cornflour
good shake black pepper	7 g ($\frac{1}{4}$ oz) butter

Wash and scrub the mussels and put them in a large saucepan with the onion, parsley, thyme, pepper, lemon juice, wine and 150 ml ($\frac{1}{2}$ pint) water. Cover and cook rapidly for 5 minutes, shaking the pan from time to time until the mussels open. Transfer the mussels to a hot, deep dish. Strain the liquid to remove any grit that may have come out of the mussels. Blend the cornflour with 2 tablespoons water, add to the fish liquid and bring to the boil, stirring all the time. Stir in the butter. Serve the mussels on deep plates and ladle the liquid over them.   *Serves 4.*

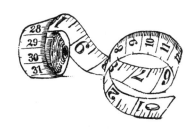

MULLIGATAWNY

Quickly prepared curried soup garnished with soured cream and chives

Here's a hot soup that can be prepared in no time at all. Sometimes you find you must stretch dinner for an extra guest. If you have already decided to serve a starter, this soup can be served as the second of four courses. The recipe is for four but, if your larder is well stocked, you can double it up in a trice. Buy a superior consommé for this recipe.

Calories: 70

342 ml (12 fl. oz) can vegetable juice

425 g (15 oz) can ready-to-serve beef consommé

$\frac{1}{4}$ teaspoon fresh curry powder

4 tablespoons soured cream

4 teaspoons fresh or frozen chives, chopped

Combine the juice, consommé and curry powder in a saucepan. Bring to the boil, stir once, then pour into individual bowls. Top each bowl with a spoon of soured cream and a sprinkling of chives.   *Serves 4.*

NORWEGIAN HOME-CURED SALMON

Fresh home-cured salmon in brandy

Calculating the calories in this recipe is extremely difficult because the weight of the bone varies according to the size of the whole fish. It won't matter if you buy more than the recipe demands, as the brandy can be made to stretch a little further and the left-overs can be stored for a few days in the refrigerator. I don't think it is worth preserving less than $1\frac{1}{2}$ lbs. The taste of this salmon is rather richer than, but certainly similar to, smoked salmon, and the fish will go further if the cured slices are beaten flat before serving.

This makes a delightful main course for a summer dinner if you offer a slightly larger portion to the others.

Calories per 50 g (2 oz) portion: 150
Calories per 75 g (3 oz) portion: 215

¾ kg (1½ lbs) middle cut of large fresh salmon
2 teaspoons salt
½ teaspoon sugar

2 tablespoons dried dill weed
6 tablespoons brandy

Cut through the outside of the salmon steak until the knife reaches the bone. Work the knife down one side between the bone and the flesh, then repeat with the other side. Remove the bone. You will now have two large fillets. To remove the skin, place the fillet skin-side down on a board and slide the knife between the skin and the flesh (as you would skin a plaice fillet). Rinse the fillets in cold water and pat dry with kitchen paper. Rub the fish with the salt and sugar mixed together, then slice thinly. Arrange the pieces, well coated with the dill weed, in a shallow dish in layers. Pour the brandy over the top, cover with cling film and then with a piece of foil. Put in the refrigerator, weighting the fish down with any dish that happens to be handy. Every 12 hours turn the fish slices over and replace the covers. Serve after 2 or 3 days.   *Serves 6 to 8.*

PEACH OVERTURE

Fresh peaches filled with curd cheese, cucumber and creamy dressing – covered in a nest of shredded lettuce

Make sure the cheese is absolutely fresh for this sunny summer starter. Stale cheese develops a 'coat' and tastes bitter. For a change, substitute cottage cheese and add chopped sweet red pepper to the mixture.

Calories: 75

2 large peaches
75 g (3 oz) curd cheese
2 tablespoons low-calorie
    salad dressing
1 tablespoon single cream
2 in. chunk cucumber,
    skinned and finely diced

small piece from lettuce
    heart, very finely
    shredded
2 boxes cress, washed and
    dried

Dip the peaches in boiling water for a few moments. **Rub** away their skins. Rinse the skinned peaches in cold water to cool, then halve, remove the stones and lay peach halves hollow side up. Beat the cheese, salad dressing and cream together, then stir in the cucumber. Pile the mixture on top of the peaches. Top with a nest of shredded lettuce and arrange on a bed of cress. Refrigerate for $\frac{1}{2}$ hour before serving. *Serves 4.*

PINK PRAWN DIP

Extravagantly attractive whole prawns surrounding a dip of tomato-flavoured yogurt pepped up with Tabasco sauce

Prawns are often used in slimmers' dishes because of their very low calorific value, but they are only eye-catching when seen cooked in their shells – large, pink and extravagant. They are usually sold by the pound but some fishmongers use a metal pint measure. You will need $1\frac{1}{2}$ pints for this recipe – you should get about sixty fish for this amount.

Calories: 60

4 tablespoons natural, low-
fat yogurt
2 tablespoons tomato
purée

5 drops Tabasco pepper
sauce
1 drop liquid sweetener
½ kg (1 lb) cooked,
unshelled prawns

Combine all the ingredients except the prawns and blend
thoroughly. Put in a small bowl standing in the centre of a
round display dish (preferably stainless steel). Arrange the
prawns, tails outwards, in a circle round the edge of the
dish. *Serves 4.*

SALAD ALEXANDER

*Individual scallop shells filled with lettuce, walnuts, pineapple,
apple and celery, blended with mango chutney and garnished
with strips of ham*

This is a fruity, light, yet substantial, starter, which uses
home-made yogurt. The recipe for yogurt on page 153,
using long-life milk and low-fat milk granules, produces a
soft, creamy texture. You should try all the brands of
natural yogurt as they vary considerably in both flavour
and texture and, if you intend to use yogurt frequently in
your slimming recipes, a change from time to time will be
appreciated.

Calories: 160

1 lettuce heart
10 walnut halves
100 g (4 oz, 2 slices) fresh
pineapple
1 apple
4 celery stalks

150 ml (¼ pint) home-made,
cream yogurt (*see page
153*)
1 teaspoon curry powder
1 teaspoon mango chutney
75 g (3 oz, 3 thin slices)
Parma ham

Shred the lettuce and divide between four dishes or scallop shells. Chop the walnuts and pineapple. Core and chop the apple and thinly slice the celery stalks. Blend the yogurt, curry powder and chutney and combine with the previously prepared ingredients. Pile the mixture on to the lettuce. Cut the ham into thin strips and arrange in a lattice pattern on top. *Serves 4.*

TOMATO AND BACON SOUP

Hot tomato soup flavoured with bacon

Whether tomatoes are canned or fresh, their calorific value is the same, but the fresh kind definitely give a better flavour to this soup. I used fresh chicken stock, well skimmed and with the fat removed instead of salty stock cubes, because the recipe contains bacon, which is itself salty. The bacon meat may be strained off to save a few more calories.

Calories: 90

50 g (2 oz) back bacon, rind and fat removed
1 onion
1 small green pepper, cored and seeded
2 celery stalks
$\frac{1}{2}$ kg (1 lb, about 8) ripe tomatoes
$\frac{1}{2}$ l (1 pint) fresh chicken stock
pepper
salt if necessary

Snip the bacon into small pieces with a pair of scissors and chop the onion, pepper and celery roughly. Put into a large saucepan with the tomatoes and the chicken stock. Bring to the boil, skim, then lower the heat and simmer until the vegetables are soft – about 30 to 40 minutes. Strain into a bowl, then blend the bacon and vegetables in a liquidizer. Pour through a fine strainer back into the saucepan and add the soup. Add pepper to taste and also add salt sparingly. Bring back to the boil, then pour into a tureen. *Serves 4.*

TOMATO COCOTTES

A garlicky mixture of tomato, egg yolks and Parmesan stuffed in a tomato shell, baked and served on a wholemeal croûte

I have quite decided that, if I were ever consigned to that desert island and had to exist on a single food, it would have to be tomatoes. Of course calories would hardly be relevant. However, while I continue to occupy the civilized world, I shall include plenty of tomatoes in my diet. There are so many ways you can prepare them. Always choose the type you need for the job in hand. Small, barely red tomatoes have a piquant, fresh taste, but, if you want them for soups, you should ask for cooking tomatoes. The green-grocer may have a box where he puts all the overripe ones, and the price will be half or less. For the following recipe buy large, firm tomatoes. Don't be afraid to use garlic as it improves the flavour no end. For non-slimmers only, butter the bread before baking.

Calories: 170

4 large firm tomatoes
1 small clove garlic, crushed
½ teaspoon salt
2 tablespoons tomato purée

4 teaspoons double cream
4 large egg yolks
4 teaspoons grated Parmesan cheese
4 slices wholemeal bread

Remove a slice from the top of each tomato from where the curve begins to straighten out. Scoop the pulp and seeds into a small bowl using a teaspoon. Brush the inside of the tomato shells with garlic mixed with salt. Turn upside down and leave to drain. Combine the tomato purée, cream and a tablespoon of the pulp. Put an egg yolk into each tomato shell, spoon the pulp mixture over the top, sprinkle with Parmesan cheese and put in a dish that just fits the tomatoes. Bake in a moderate oven (180°C, 350°F, Gas 4) for $\frac{1}{2}$ hour. Using a fluted pastry cutter, press out a circle from each slice of bread. Spread these circles out on a non-stick baking tray and put them in the oven for the last 15 minutes of the cooking time to dry out. To serve, top each piece of bread with a stuffed tomato. *Serves 4.*

2
Fish

BAKED RED MULLET

Baked in papillotes and served with maître d'hôtel butter

Because it has such an attractive red skin, red mullet may be served simply grilled or baked at even the smartest dinner party. You may have to hunt around to find it, and it is expensive, but the flavour is exquisite and the roes are much prized. Red mullet is a summer-season fish so you can serve it hot or cold with salad. Tiny dice of boiled potato and raw peeled cucumber, tossed in a sauce of low-fat skimmed-milk cheese mixed with a tablespoon of low-calorie salad dressing, would make an attractive garnish.

Calories (without maître d'hôtel butter) : 220

4 × 225 g (8 oz) red mullet	pepper
25 g (1 oz) butter	lemon juice
salt	*maître d'hôtel* butter

Scrape the fish the way of the grain to remove the large scales, but leave the skin unblemished. Cut off the gills and fins, slit the belly just underneath the head and remove the gut, but not the liver. Do not remove the head. Rub the fish lightly with butter and season with salt, pepper and a sprinkling of lemon juice. Wrap each fish separately in non-stick paper. Place them on a baking tray and bake in a moderate oven (180°C, 350°F, Gas 4) for about 20 minutes, then open one packet and test with a sharp knife on the underside. When they are done, unwrap the cooked fish and arrange on a heated serving dish. Hand round *maître d'hôtel* butter separately so that the slimmer can push it to one side before it melts. *Serves 4.*

MAÎTRE D'HÔTEL BUTTER

Maître d'hôtel butter will keep in the freezer for about one month. Since it can be served with any grilled fish or meat, you might care to make up a larger quantity than immediately required. Allow 15 g ($\frac{1}{2}$ oz) butter per average serving, but this could be stretched to a mere 7 g ($\frac{1}{4}$ oz) sliver.

Calories: 115

50 g (2 oz) good-quality   salt
   butter   pepper
2 teaspoons fresh parsley   few drops fresh lemon juice
   very finely chopped

Beat the butter until soft and work in the remaining ingredients. Form into a sausage shape and roll up evenly in a piece of damp greaseproof paper. Twist the ends in cracker fashion. Chill until firm, then unwrap and slice evenly. *Serves 4.*

COMPÔTE OF HADDOCK

Bite-sized pieces of fresh fish cooked in a saffron stock with potatoes, tomatoes and onions and thickened with egg yolk

Although the flavour of cod would be just as good as that of haddock, cod is unsuitable in this recipe because it is imperative to use the head and bones of the fish to enrich the stew. The smallest cod weighs about 6 lbs but whole haddock can be as small as 1 lb. As I am suggesting using fish of about 3 lbs, this rules out cod. As this is a peasant-style dish, the herbs should be left in the dish for your guests to remove themselves.

Calories : 230 per person

1 whole, fresh haddock
   weighing 1½ kg (3½ lbs)
3 large cloves garlic,
   bruised
798 g (28 oz) can tomatoes
3 large onions, thinly sliced
450 g (1 lb) potatoes,
   peeled
3 bay leaves

4 sprigs thyme
4 sprigs parsley
1 sprig rosemary
salt
pepper
few strands saffron
2 egg yolks
4 tablespoons skimmed
   milk

Remove the head, bones and skin from the fish and wrap them in muslin with the garlic. Tie securely. You will probably have to cut the backbone into three or four pieces. Put muslin bag in a saucepan with 1·2 l (2 pints) water and add the tomatoes, onions and the potatoes, cut into walnut-sized pieces. Add the herbs and a little salt and pepper. Bring to the boil, then lower the heat and simmer for precisely 20 minutes. (Prolonged cooking of the bones is inclined to give a bitter taste.) Remove the muslin bag, pressing it against the side of the pan with a fork to extract all the juices. Taste the liquid and add more salt if necessary.

Cut the fish into large chunks and add to the pan with a few strands of saffron. Cover and cook very gently until the fish is opaque and flaky – about 15 to 20 minutes. Remove from the heat, cool rapidly and refrigerate overnight. Reheat the compôte just before serving and, when it is hot but not boiling, stir in the egg yolks blended with the milk. Take off the heat at once and pour into a heated tureen. *Serves 6.*

COQUILLES ST JACQUES TROUVILLE

Scallops and tomatoes in a creamy sauce – served in the fish shells and garnished with a border of potato (optional), then sprinkled with breadcrumbs and browned under the grill

Why should low-calorie scallops poached in water and coated in a modest amount of white sauce produce a recipe that is so high in calories? The answer is that the potato border makes up practically half the calories in this dish (130 each). Therefore, why not cheat a little and pipe a thick border for the others and a thin one for yourself? The quantities given should fill the scallop shells, making this dish ideal for a main course.

Calories: 200 (slimmer's portion, without potato)

8 scallops
½ onion, roughly chopped
salt
white pepper
1 teaspoon lemon juice
1 bay leaf
3 tomatoes
25 g (1 oz) butter
2 tablespoons flour
150 ml (¼ pint) skimmed milk
1 tablespoon single cream
350 g (12 oz) hot, creamy mashed potatoes
2 tablespoons dried breadcrumbs
4 greased deep scallop shells

Wash the scallops, making sure you remove all the grit. Put in a saucepan with the onion, a generous shake of salt and pepper, the lemon juice and the bay leaf. Add 150 ml ($\frac{1}{4}$ pint) water, then cook gently for 5 to 6 minutes, never allowing the water to boil. Strain, reserving the liquid. Skin the tomatoes by immersing in boiling water for a minute or so. Cut them in half, scoop out the pips and slice the flesh into thin strips. In another saucepan melt the butter and blend in the flour. Cook over gentle heat for 1 minute, then whisk in the reserved liquid and milk. Bring to the boil, whisking all the time. Remove from the heat, adjust the seasoning and stir in the cream. Cut up the scallops and arrange them in the scallop shells with the tomato strips. Pour the sauce over, pipe a border of potato around the edges and sprinkle the breadcrumbs over the sauce. Brown under the grill.   *Serves 4.*

CRAB AND CUCUMBER LAYERED CRÊPES

Twelve wafer-thin pancakes stacked one on top of the other, filled with layers of creamy crabmeat and garnished with soft cheese and chopped prawns

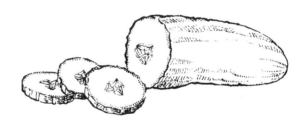

A crêpe is a very thin pancake. Thick pancakes would spoil this dish because, when stacked, they tend to be solid. For the non-slimmers, serve mayonnaise thinned down with single cream.

Calories: 150 (for $\frac{1}{6}$ of the cake)

Batter

100 g (4 oz) plain flour	300 ml ($\frac{1}{2}$ pint) skimmed
pinch salt	milk
1 large egg	1 teaspoon vegetable oil

Filling

185 g (6$\frac{1}{2}$ oz) can crabmeat	50 g (2 oz) skimmed-milk
$\frac{1}{2}$ small cucumber	soft cheese
8 small gherkins	pinch mustard powder

Garnish

25 g (1 oz) skimmed-milk soft cheese	50 g (2 oz) prawns, finely chopped

Make up the pancake batter in the usual way, by beating together all the ingredients except the oil. Drain the crabmeat, peel and dice the cucumber and slice the gherkins. Mix with the cheese and mustard. Brush a non-stick pan with the oil; then, without further greasing, make twelve wafer-thin pancakes, keeping each warm until they are all cooked. Layer the pancakes on a heated platter with some crabmeat filling between each. Spread a $\frac{1}{2}$ in. border of cheese around the top pancake and place the prawns on top. Cut into wedges and serve immediately on heated individual plates. *Serves 4 to 6.*

CRAB SOUFFLÉ

A glorious soufflé of crabmeat and mushrooms, with white wine and a trace of curry flavour

Those who are clever at soufflé-making cannot understand why the rest of us fail. Here are some tips: make sure you use a straight-sided soufflé dish, well greased so that the mixture can glide majestically up the sides; do not have the oven too hot or the outside will set quickly, forming a lid which prevents the remainder of the mixture from rising;

and leave the soufflé to cook peacefully for the first 20 minutes or preferably longer before inspecting.

Calories: 420

1 shallot, finely chopped
1 tablespoon vegetable oil
50 g (2 oz) button
　　mushrooms, cut into
　　quarters
3 tablespoons white wine
1 tablespoon tomato purée
1 tablespoon curry powder

250 g (9 oz) crabmeat,
　　finely chopped
50 g (2 oz) butter
50 g·(2 oz) flour
300 ml ($\frac{1}{2}$ pint) milk
salt
pepper
4 size 2 eggs, separated

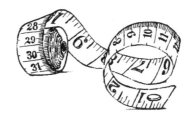

Preheat a moderate oven (180°C, 350°F, Gas 4) and place a shelf in the centre, allowing plenty of space above for the soufflé to rise. Brown the shallot in the oil, add the mushrooms and cook for another minute or two. Add the wine, tomato purée, curry powder and crabmeat and stir over gentle heat until the liquid has evaporated. In another saucepan prepare a thick white sauce with the butter, flour and milk. Season well. Leave the sauce to cool for a few minutes, then stir in the beaten egg yolks. Beat the egg whites until fairly stiff when the peaks just tip over. Combine the crabmeat mixture with the sauce, then fold in the beaten egg whites, first stirring in one spoonful of the whites to open out the texture. Pour into a greased 7 inch soufflé dish so that the mixture reaches only three-quarters of the way up the sides. Bake for 25 to 35 minutes until the soufflé is well risen and golden on top. Serve at once.　*Serves 4.*

DIJON HADDOCK

The mingled flavour of shallots, onions and leeks, sautéed with fish, then poached gently and spiced with mustard

Shallots, which taste like onions with a slightly garlicky flavour, are a necessary ingredient of this dish, but, if you have decided nevertheless to only use onions, choose pickling onions, which are available in the autumn, or the smallest onions you can obtain, and add a crushed clove of garlic. The onions remain whole in this recipe so it is important to avoid those with shrivelled skins or soft necks – indications that they are going bad. To retain firmness, buy one large haddock fillet rather than two or three small ones.

Calories (without potato border) : 205

675 g (1½ lbs) fresh haddock fillet, skinned
6 shallots
10 baby onions
4 × 1 in. thick leeks, white part only
1 tablespoon vegetable oil
4 tablespoons tomato purée
salt
pepper
1 tablespoon French mustard
175 g (6 oz) hot mashed potato

Remove any remaining bones and cut the fish into large chunks which will hold their shape during cooking. Peel the shallots and onions and chop the leeks very finely. Heat the oil in a large pan and fry the shallots, onions and leeks for 4 to 5 minutes until golden and softening. Gently add the fish, cooking for a further minute or two and turning until the flesh is opaque. Add barely enough hot water to cover, then stir in the tomato purée and seasoning to taste. Cover with a lid and cook very gently for ½ to ¾ hour until the onions are tender. Remove a little of the hot liquid, blend with the mustard, pour back into the pan, stir and reheat. Pour contents of the pan into a heated serving dish and pipe a border of potato round the edge. *Serves 4.*

FISH GRATINÉE

A bake of minced fish, basil, courgettes and tomatoes, topped with grated Edam cheese and breadcrumbs

Some fishmongers, particularly those with a large Jewish clientèle, sell freshly minced fish. Use this for *Gefülte* fish, quickly prepared fish balls or fish cakes. If your local trader doesn't give this service, and you have to do your own mincing, remember to remove the skin and bones before you start or you will find disconcerting crunchy bits in your food. It is best to use a variety of white fish in this dish including a little of the delicately flavoured bream.

Calories: 180

6 tomatoes	1 teaspoon basil
1 onion, chopped	salt
450 g (1 lb) minced white fish fillet	pepper
	450 g (1 lb) courgettes

50 g (2 oz) grated Edam cheese
2 tablespoons dry breadcrumbs } mixed together

Skin the tomatoes by immersing in boiling water for a few minutes, then chop. Mix the onion and tomato with the fish, basil and seasoning. Top, tail and thinly slice the courgettes and arrange them in alternate layers with the fish in a greased casserole. Cover with a lid and bake in a moderate oven (180°C, 350°F, Gas 4) until tender – about 1½ hours. Remove the lid, sprinkle with cheese and crumbs, raise the heat to 200°C, 400°F, Gas 6 and bake for a further 15 minutes until browned. *Serves 4.*

FISH IN SOUR CREAM SAUCE

Sliced tomatoes, fresh haddock and tarragon combined with cream, onion, ham and cheese and baked until bubbling

Edam is one of the low-calorie cheeses but, if it is one of your favourites, make sure that you buy exactly 100 g (4 oz) and don't leave any for nibbling. Use a steel knife to pare away the inedible waxy rind, as the colour is difficult to remove from a stainless steel knife.

Calories: 285

½ kg (1 lb) firm tomatoes
350 g (12 oz) fresh haddock
  fillet, skinned
1 teaspoon tarragon leaves
150 ml (¼ pint) soured
  cream
1 medium onion, finely
  chopped

100 g (4 oz) lean boiled
  ham, finely chopped
100 g (4 oz) Edam cheese,
  grated
salt
pepper

Slice the tomatoes thickly and spread out in the base of a shallow, greased, ovenproof dish. Put the fish in a frying pan, just cover with water and poach until opaque. Drain thoroughly, then flake and spread over the tomatoes. Sprinkle the tarragon on top. Combine the cream, onion, ham and three-quarters of the cheese and season with salt and pepper. Spoon over the fish and sprinkle with the remaining cheese. Bake uncovered in a moderate oven (180°C, 350°F, Gas 4) for 15 to 20 minutes until bubbling and brown on top. Serve hot with mange-tout, diced carrots and green beans. *Serves 4.*

FILLET OF SOLE CECILIA

Fillets of Dover sole with asparagus tips and cheese

The title has nothing to do with my name – it is purely coincidental. Traditionally 'Cecilia' describes fish gently cooked in butter and garnished with asparagus tips and grated cheese. Use a non-stick frying pan to help brown the fish. Obviously it will not be possible to sauté all the fish at the same time, so start with half the butter and oil, adding the remainder when cooking the second batch.

Calories: 250

4 × 350 g (12 oz) Dover soles, skinned and filleted
salt
pepper
25 g (1 oz) butter

1 tablespoon vegetable oil
283 g (10 oz) can asparagus tips, drained
50 g (2 oz) Cheddar cheese, finely grated

Cut the fillets of sole in half lengthwise and season with salt and pepper. Sauté gently in the butter and oil, turning the fillets over once. Arrange in a double layer in a flameproof dish. Cover with the asparagus tips and sprinkle with cheese. Brown briefly under a hot grill. *Serves 4.*

GRILLED MACKEREL WITH GOOSEBERRY SAUCE

An old English recipe brought up to date

Mackerel are relatively cheap fish with silvery-blue, very shiny skins and firm flesh. Press them with your thumbs to make sure they are fresh. They should be resilient to the touch. If you intend to purée the gooseberries in the liquid-izer, they must be topped and tailed first, otherwise you will find big brown specks staring out from the sauce.

Calories: 210

225 g (8 oz) gooseberries, fresh or frozen
1 tablespoon caster sugar
1 teaspoon grated lemon rind
few drops liquid sweetener (optional)

4 × 225 to 275 g (8 to 10 oz) mackerel
salt
pepper
1 tablespoon vegetable oil
gooseberry or raspberry leaves to garnish

Simmer the gooseberries in about 150 ml ($\frac{1}{4}$ pint) water until tender, then rub through a sieve. Stir in the sugar, lemon rind and sweetener, if used. Season the inside of the mackerel with salt and pepper and brush the skin with oil. Grill for 6 to 7 minutes on each side, then transfer them to a heated serving dish. Reheat the sauce and pour it over the fish. Garnish the dish with washed fruit leaves, but do not serve them as they are inedible. *Serves 4.*

HALIBUT À L'ÉSTRAGON

Halibut marinated in fresh tarragon and lemon juice, then simply grilled

Who can tell whether halibut will be tasty or watery when cooked? I certainly can't and when I asked advice from a reliable fishmonger he said that he could never be sure himself but suggested that the longer the fish is stored on ice, the more the flavour disappears. Ideally, sautéed potatoes and petits pois should be served with this dish, but these potatoes are out for the slimmer (there are 70 calories in one walnut-sized piece) and it is better to say 'no thank you' altogether, rather than trying to restrict yourself to one piece, as they are so more-ish.

Calories: 280

bunch fresh tarragon   salt
2 lemons   pepper
675 g (1½ lbs) halibut fillet 1 tablespoon vegetable oil

Spread half the tarragon and the juice of one lemon in a long shallow dish. Season both sides of the fish with salt and pepper, place it in the dish and cover with the remaining tarragon and lemon juice. Leave to marinate for 5 to 6 hours, occasionally spooning the juice over the fish. Remove the fish, brush with the oil and, depending on the thickness of the fish, grill for 4 to 5 minutes on each side, basting with the juices from time to time.   *Serves 4.*

ORANGE-BUTTERED PLAICE

Plaice fillets cooked with orange-flavoured butter

Leave the skins on the fish fillets. The fillets look larger that way and your guests may choose not to eat them, which will certainly save them a few calories. When buying plaice fillets you will find that the cost is the same whether they are cut from a whole fish by the fishmonger or sold ready filleted. Sniff the fish if you can and, if it smells unduly strong or looks grey, do not buy it. Only the best quality should be used in this recipe. June to January are best months for plaice.

Calories: 250

1 orange   salt
50 g (2 oz) butter   pepper
4 × 150 g (5 oz) plaice
    fillets – or 1 kg (2¼ lbs)
    whole fish, filleted

Grate the orange rind and squeeze out the juice. Beat into the butter the rind and as much juice as it will absorb.

Form into a sausage shape, wrap in a Christmas cracker of greaseproof paper and freeze until firm. Sprinkle the flesh side of the fish with salt and pepper, then, using a potato peeler, cover sparingly with grated butter. This should need only about a quarter of the butter but grate the remainder and offer separately. Bake at 180°C, 350°F, Gas 4 for 15 minutes until the fish appears deliciously white and soft. *Serves 4.*

PLAICE ÉLAINE

A mélange *of crab, lobster, prawns and shrimps tossed in butter and piled on to baked plaice fillets*

A small crab weighs ½ kg (1 lb) and when boiled the yield of edible meat is only about 70 g (2¾ oz). Don't ask the fishmonger to dress it for you as he will probably put breadcrumbs in the mixture. But you could ask him to open the crab and remove the 'dead men's fingers'. Both crab and lobster meat are obtainable frozen.

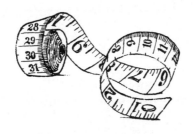

Calories: 225

4 × 175 g (6 oz) thick, white-skinned plaice fillets	15 g (½ oz) butter
	¼ teaspoon cayenne
	¼ teaspoon ground nutmeg
lemon juice	freshly ground white pepper
75 g (3 oz) crabmeat	
75 g (3 oz) lobster meat	salt
100 g (4 oz) peeled prawns	lemon slices to garnish
50 g (2 oz) peeled shrimps	

Sprinkle the plaice fillets with lemon juice and arrange in a single layer on a baking tray lined with non-stick paper. Cover with a 'tent' of foil to prevent sticking and bake in a moderate oven (180°C, 350°F, Gas 4) for 20 to 25 minutes. Meanwhile chop the crabmeat, lobster meat and prawns, but leave the shrimps whole. Melt the butter in a non-stick pan, add the seasonings and the shellfish, tossing gently until thoroughly heated. To serve, arrange the plaice fillets on a heated large round dish, tails towards the centre. Pile the shellfish in the centre and garnish the edges of the dish with halved lemon slices. *Serves 4.*

POACHED TROUT WITH LEMON THYME

Trout gently cooked in an aromatic sauce of green peppercorns, fresh herbs, onion and white wine

It goes without saying that trout come in different sizes depending on at what age they are caught. Count 35 calories an ounce for the whole trout including the head and bones etc. The weight will be printed on the sides of a packet of frozen trout and may be as low as 175 g (6 oz) or as high as 350 g (12 oz). For a main course serve three large fish for the non-slimmers and one small for yourself. I have used 225 g (8 oz) fish in this recipe. If you decide to cook the fish from their frozen state, double the simmering time.

Calories: 290 (butter pats: 60 each)

4 × 225 g (8 oz) trout, gutted but with head on
salt
6 green peppercorns
6 sprigs lemon thyme (or 1 teaspoon dried thyme if you have no choice)

1 small onion, thinly sliced
1 lemon, thinly sliced
150 ml ($\frac{1}{4}$ pint) dry white wine
4 g ($\frac{1}{4}$ oz) butter pats to garnish

Sprinkle the trout with salt and put them in a large frying pan or sturdy roasting tin. Add the peppercorns, thyme, onion and lemon. Pour the wine over, adding just sufficient water to cover the trout. Heat to simmering point and cook for 6 to 8 minutes, turning the fish over gently once. Remove the fish carefully, using two fish slices and let all the liquid drain away. Arrange on a heated serving dish and pop a pat of frozen butter on top so that it may be removed by the slimmer before it melts. *Serves 4.*

SALMON ROYALE

Middle-cut fresh salmon poached in a court bouillon, covered with prawns and scallops in a bland sauce and topped with caviar

A luxury salmon and seafood dish topped with caviar. Rather expensive but a memorable dish for the frustrated slimmer. Serve hot, or spoon shellfish mixture over the salmon when cold. Although it has 450 calories a portion, this dish would only require a light salad accompaniment.

Calories: 450

4 × 175 g (6 oz) middle-cut darnes of salmon
4 scallops removed from shell
court bouillon
150 ml (5 fl. oz) natural, low-fat yogurt
1 tablespoon low-calorie salad cream
1 tablespoon double cream
100 g (4 oz) peeled prawns
15 g (½ oz) caviar

Put the salmon and scallops in a large saucepan, cover with court bouillon and poach gently for 10 to 15 minutes. Drain thoroughly. Combine the yogurt, salad cream and double cream in a warmed bowl. Mix in the prawns and the scallops cut into quarters. Arrange the salmon on a serving dish. Spoon some shellfish mixture on each piece and top with caviar. *Serves 4.*

To make the court bouillon: Place one sliced onion, one thinly sliced small carrot, 2 tablespoons malt vinegar, 2 bay leaves, salt and pepper in a large pan with 1 l (1¾ pints) cold water. Bring to the boil and simmer for 10 minutes. Cool and strain. Cook the salmon in the cold court bouillon.

SAVOURY SALMON CHEESECAKE

An unusual cheesecake made of cottage cheese, salmon and tomatoes on a savoury-biscuit base

A spring or summer dish which you can serve as a starter or main course, with a selection of salads or as an after-dinner savoury. While not wishing to discriminate, I imagine the gentlemen might prefer not to have this as a main course but the ladies would appreciate it. I used MacVities Kracka Wheat biscuits because they crush easily and form a softer base than crispbread.

Calories: 390 (for a starter portion)

50 g (2 oz) butter
100 g (4 oz, 16) Kracka
　Wheat biscuits, finely
　crushed
15 g (½ oz) powdered
　gelatine
350 g (12 oz) cottage
　cheese
2 tablespoons natural low-
　fat yogurt

red food colouring
2 small tomatoes, skinned,
　seeded and chopped
99 g (3½ oz) can pink
　salmon, drained and
　flaked
1 tablespoon freshly
　chopped parsley
salt
pepper

For garnish
1 box cress
cucumber slices
tomato slices

Melt the butter, mix in the biscuits and press the mixture into the base of a 6 in. loose-bottomed cake tin. Refrigerate until firm. Dissolve the gelatine in 4 tablespoons hot water, then mix with the cheese and yogurt and blend in the liquidizer with 2 drops red food colour. Turn into a bowl and fold in the tomatoes, salmon, parsley and seasoning. Pour this mixture into the cake tin over the biscuit base. Refrigerate for 1 hour or until set. Push the cake out of the tin and, without removing the tin bottom, place it in the centre of a round serving platter. Surround with a border of cress to conceal the metal rim. Arrange overlapping rings of cucumber and tomato in a circle on top of the cake. *Serves 8.*

SCAMPI KEBABS

Cubes of aubergine, green peppers, scampi and pearl onions sprinkled with lemon juice and grilled until tender

Scampi should be large prawns caught in Dublin Bay, but the real things are not easy to obtain. Substitute the largest Pacific prawns available. You may well find, when you are eating out, that you are given a plate of small pieces of white fish, crumbed and fried as a good disguise. Thread the scampi on to skewers while still nearly frozen and they will stay moist throughout cooking.

Calories: 145

1 medium aubergine
1 medium green pepper
salt
450 g (1 lb) peeled frozen
    scampi, barely thawed

8 pearl onions
2 tablespoons fresh lemon
    juice

Peel the aubergine, cut into quarters lengthwise and then into 1 in. cubes. Core and seed the pepper and cut into similarly sized pieces. Half fill a large saucepan with water, stir in a teaspoon of salt and the aubergines. Bring to the boil and simmer for 3 minutes, then add the peppers. Continue cooking for another 2 minutes. Drain thoroughly and leave to cool before threading on to the skewers with the scampi and onions. Sprinkle the kebabs with lemon juice and cook under a preheated grill for about 10 minutes, turning during grilling so that all sides are evenly cooked. *Serves 4.*

SEAFOOD ALICE J. DORTCH

A mushroom fondue dip with peeled shrimps and dressed crab

The United Daughters of the Confederacy is a women's organization somewhat like our WI. The original recipe came from a Chapter in Mississippi where shrimp and crab is very popular. Serve with hot rice, green salad and crispy Melba toast (25 calories for one triangle).

Calories: 175

298 g (10½ oz) can condensed cream of mushroom soup

100 g (4 oz) button mushrooms, sliced

4 spring onions, thinly sliced

2 tablespoons finely chopped parsley

½ teaspoon paprika

½ teaspoon freshly ground black pepper

225 g (8 oz) peeled shrimps

71 g (2½ oz) can dressed crab

150 ml (5 fl. oz) natural, low-fat yogurt

Warm the soup, add the mushrooms, onions, parsley, paprika and pepper. Cook gently without boiling for 5 minutes. Add the shrimps and crabmeat and bring to just below boiling point. The mixture will be quite thick at this stage. Stir in the yogurt and immediately remove from the heat. Pour into a chafing dish set over a tiny flame and set in the middle of the table. Allow guests to help themselves.

To make Melba toast, toast medium-thick ready-sliced bread and, immediately each slice is ready, cut off the crusts and slide a sharp-bladed knife horizontally through the centre. Halve each piece diagonally and toast the uncooked sides. *Serves 4.*

SMOKED HADDOCK AND POTATO RAMEKINS

Individual dishes of smoked haddock, potato and cheese mousse – baked in a thick white sauce and cooked similarly to a soufflé

The colour of the flesh is no indication of the flavour of smoked haddock or cod. Manufacturers get up to all sorts of tricks and sometimes the fish has been nowhere near the smoke. If you are buying frozen packs, look for the word 'smoked' on the label. As fish is the most important ingredient in this dish, it is worth while choosing carefully. If you have a friendly fishmonger, ask his advice. The calories have been calculated on the weight of fish after skinning and boning. Skin may weigh 2 to 3 oz and a large backbone 3 to 3½ oz.

Calories: 190

575 g (1¼ lbs) smoked haddock
275 g (10 oz) boiled and mashed potato
65 g (2½ oz) strong Cheddar cheese, finely grated

6 tablespoons skimmed milk
3 size 1 egg yolks
6 size 1 egg whites
salt
pepper

Grease six individual ramekin dishes and prepare a moderate oven (180°C, 350°F, Gas 4). Poach the fish in water for about 8 minutes until the flesh is opaque, then drain thoroughly and remove the skin and bones. Flake the fish and mix with the potato, cheese, milk and egg yolks. Beat thoroughly until smooth and the consistency of thick sauce. Don't use a liquidizer or the mixture may become waxy. Beat the egg whites until stiff but not dry. Stir one tablespoon of the beaten egg whites into the fish sauce, then fold in the remainder of the egg whites. Half fill the ramekin dishes with the mixture and bake for 15 minutes before opening the oven door to inspect. Cook for a further 5 minutes if necessary, when the ramekin should be well risen and brown on top. Serve with a green salad and French beans.   *Serves 5 to 6.*

SOLE ROSSOVERDE

Whole Dover sole baked in the oven and garnished with an asparagus and prawn sauce

Dover sole, expensive though it is, lends itself to extravagant entertaining – the steak of the fish world. The firm flesh holds easily on the fork – important if your guests come from a country where it is customary to eat with this single implement. The fish skins are added to enrich the sauce, but are not served.

Calories: 240

4 × 350 g (¾ lb) Dover
   soles, heads removed
150 ml (¼ pint) sweet white
   wine
1 tablespoon lemon juice
salt

pepper
283 g (10 oz) can asparagus
   tips
1 oz butter
2 tablespoons flour
100 g (4 oz) peeled prawns

Skin the fish and tuck the skins in a corner of a greased roasting tin. Arrange the fish in the tin in a single layer. Mix the wine, lemon juice, salt and pepper with 150 ml ($\frac{1}{4}$ pint) water and pour over the fish. Cover with greased foil and bake in a moderate oven (180°C, 350°F, Gas 4) for 25 to 30 minutes. Remove the fish to a heated serving dish and strain the liquid into a saucepan. Add to this any liquid from the drained asparagus. Combine the butter and flour in a cup or small bowl, mixing to a soft ball. Bring the fish liquid to the boil and gradually whisk in small pieces of the butter mixture. When the sauce has thickened, adjust the seasoning. Add the asparagus, folding in gently, then carefully spoon it over the fish and sprinkle with prawns. *Serves 4.*

TALAVIERA SCALLOPS

A casserole of white fish, onions and tomato blended with tomato purée and port and mellowed with cream

When fresh scallops are not available, substitute the frozen variety. You will need 450 g (1 lb) for this recipe. Since this dish is a real 'calorie bargain', the slimmer may have her fair share of boiled rice or mashed potato.

Calories: 210

225 g (8 oz) fresh white fish fillet, skinned
8 scallops, washed
15 g ($\frac{1}{2}$ oz) flour
salt
pepper
1 medium onion, finely chopped

2 tomatoes, peeled and chopped
2 teaspoons tomato purée
4 tablespoons port
4 tablespoons soured cream
freshly chopped parsley

Cut the fish into bite-size pieces but leave the scallops whole. Toss both in the flour seasoned with salt and pepper. Spread the onions and tomato in the base of a flame-proof casserole and arrange the fish on top. Blend the tomato purée with the port and pour this over the fish. Cover and bake in a moderate oven (180°C, 350°F, Gas 4) for 25 to 30 minutes until tender. Remove the fish and boil the sauce, stirring continuously until it thickens, then adjust the seasoning. Return the fish to the sauce, reheat briefly, then switch off the heat and stir in the cream. Serve in the casserole or transfer to a heated serving dish and garnish with parsley. Serve with boiled rice or mashed potato.   *Serves 4.*

3
Meat

BEEF STROGONOFF

Strips of rump steak sealed, then cooked in a sauce of consommé, mushroom and beans, flavoured with rosemary

A whole steak on a plate will be judged by its size, and someone with a healthy appetite will scorn a 100 g (4 oz piece). So I stretch the steak by slicing thinly. This reduces both the budget and the calories in one fell swoop. As always, cut the rice right down for the poor old slimmer.

Calories (without rice): 275

450 g (1 lb) rump steak (weighed without the fatty edge)
2 tablespoons vegetable oil
1 large onion, sliced into thin rings
25 g (1 oz) flour
156 g (5½ oz) can condensed consommé
225 g (8 oz) mushrooms, washed and sliced

225 g (8 oz) French or snap beans, hulled
sprig rosemary
salt
pepper
120 ml (4 fl. oz) soured cream
225 g (8 oz) long-grain rice, freshly cooked

Trim the beef and cut into thin narrow strips. Fry briskly in the hot oil until sealed, add the onion and continue frying over medium heat until soft. Sprinkle with the flour and stir in to avoid lumps. Add the consommé, 150 ml (¼ pint) hot water, mushrooms, beans and rosemary. Cook gently until the mixture thickens. Taste and add salt and pepper. Cover with a lid and simmer for 30 to 45 minutes until the meat is cooked but not as soft as stewed steak. Stir in the soured cream and reheat, but do not boil or the sauce may curdle. Arrange the rice round the edges of a heated serving dish and pour the meat mixture into the centre. There should be no need for additional garnish. *Serves 5.*

CHINESE MUSTARD BALLS

Tiny minced beef balls flavoured with mustard, tomato purée and lemon juice – served in nests of bean sprouts and raw vegetables

My less-fat-than-she-was married daughter, always working out slimming recipes, offers this one. It was so quick and easy to prepare that she was not standing around in the kitchen for ages succumbing to the nibbling temptations while waiting for the cooking to 'happen'. Shape the meat into twenty-four small balls and serve four to yourself and more to everyone else.

Calories: 230 (special slimmer's portion)

½ kg (1 lb) bean sprouts	grated rind and juice of 1
½ green pepper, cored and	lemon
seeded	1 tablespoon tomato purée
1 carrot	1 tablespoon French
1 tomato	mustard
675 g (1½ lb) raw, lean	salt
minced beef	pepper
1 large egg	

Soak the bean sprouts in cold water for 15 minutes, then drain thoroughly. Dry on kitchen paper. Dice the green pepper and the carrot and chop the tomato. Mix with the bean sprouts and arrange nests of the mixture in individual bowls. 'Scrudle' (Dilys's word for mixing everything together without making too much fuss) the remaining ingredients and form into twenty-four small balls. Put in a roasting tin and bake without covering in a fairly hot (190°C, 375°F, Gas 5) oven for ¾ to 1 hour until nice and brown. Arrange the meat balls brown side up in the nests. *Serves 4.*

EPICUREAN SPICED BEEF

Sirloin of beef cured with crushed garlic, dark sugar and allspice, encased in luten paste and baked in a hot oven

A type of salt beef which takes about a week to cure. The quantity given will serve a generous six portions. To be sure of the calorie content, you would be advised to cut a few slices and find the weight of one. Cut wafer-thin slices for yourself. 1 oz cured beef has 85 Calories. Serve with low-calorie salads and offer boiled potatoes to the others.

Calories: 300 (slimmer's 3 oz portion)

1 kg (2¼ lb) joint of beef sirloin, trimmed and rolled
1 clove garlic, crushed
40 g (1½ oz) dark brown sugar
15 g (½ oz) ground allspice
1 teaspoon freshly ground black pepper

2 bay leaves, crumbled
50 to 75 g (2 to 3 oz) coarse salt
flour
1 tablespoon bottled fruit sauce
2 carrots, grated

Rub the joint with the crushed garlic. Combine the sugar, allspice, pepper, bay leaves and salt. Turn on to a sheet of greaseproof paper and roll the joint in the mixture until thoroughly coated. Cover to keep out the dust and put in a cold place – not in the refrigerator because the garlic smell would be absorbed by the other foodstuffs. Leave for five days. Each day rub in a little more salt. To cook, mix about 225 g (8 oz) flour with cold water to make a thick putty. Roll out big enough to encase the joint and wrap tightly. Put in a roasting tin with a few tablespoons water. Bake in a fairly hot over (190°C, 375°F, Gas 5) for $1\frac{1}{2}$ hours. Leave to cool. Remove the pastry case at the table or cut away and discard in the kitchen, garnishing the meat with a smear of fruity sauce and raw grated carrot. *Serves 6.*

GRILLED LAMB WITH CURRANT SAUCE

A delicate garnish of tomato roses set on a sauce of breadcrumbs, butter, cloves and wine enhances the plainly grilled chops

A 150 g (5 oz) lamb chop yields only half its weight of lean meat. When well grilled the 'eye' is equivalent to 140 calories. Even if you do not eat any of the fat, your guests may well enjoy at least part of it. Buy eight small, rather than four large chops, when you can restrict yourself to one only.

Calories: 240 (slimmer's single portion)

8 × 150 g (5 oz) lamb chops
75 g (3 oz) currants
50 g (2 oz) fresh
   breadcrumbs

$\frac{1}{4}$ to $\frac{1}{2}$ teaspoon ground
   cloves
4 tablespoons red wine
1 teaspoon butter
tomato roses for garnish

While grilling the chops, simmer the currants in 300 ml ($\frac{1}{2}$ pint) water for 5 minutes, then add the breadcrumbs, cloves, wine and butter to the currants. Lower the heat and cook gently until smooth – about 10 minutes. Drain the chops and arrange them, bone end out, on a heated round platter. Fill the centre with the sauce and garnish with tomato roses. *Serves 4.*

Tomato roses: The artistic person will have no difficulty in preparing attractive garnishes. The less blessed will have to practise this one. Using a sharp vegetable knife, pare the skin from a large tomato in a spiral about $\frac{1}{2}$ in. wide. Lay the skin on a board, trim one end to a point and shave the flesh from the top and bottom edges until only the outer skin remains. Curl over the pointed end once with the flesh side out, then reverse the skin and roll up to form a rose. Either seal with a clove or sew with a thread or celery string. If this is too difficult, plant the roses in cucumber beds made from a hollowed-out thick cucumber slice.

HUNGARIAN LIVER

Sautéed slivers of lamb's liver bathed in soured cream and paprika and garnished with freshly chopped parsley

Lamb's liver is the lowest calorie liver and is high in iron. Even cholesterol watchers should eat it once a week, but they, of course, should not have the sauce. At 240 calories a portion it is a suitable slimmer's food. Serve with a salad of your choice.

Calories: 240

450 g (1 lb) lamb's liver	150 ml (5 fl. oz) soured
salt	cream
pepper	1 teaspoon paprika
15 g ($\frac{1}{2}$ oz) butter	chopped parsley

Prepare a hot grill. Skin the liver, remove the membranes and slice into eight. Season with salt and pepper. Remove the grill rack and put the butter in the pan. Put under a medium grill to melt the butter, then add the liver, turning the slices over immediately. Grill for 6 to 8 minutes – until tender but not dry – turning the pieces over once during cooking. Transfer to a heated serving dish. Pour the cream into the remaining juices in the grill pan, stir in the paprika and heat for 1 minute. Pour this over the meat and sprinkle with chopped parsley. *Serves 4.*

JAMAICAN BEEF

A whole marrow filled with cubes of lean beef cooked with okra and bananas

I prefer to buy a lump of meat and trim it myself. Every vestige of fat and gristle must go and it is much easier to do this before dicing. I find that it is usually false economy to buy cheap cuts, as they may be fattier and will almost certainly be tougher and take longer to cook. The banana in this recipe gives a smooth flavour, but don't expect to see whole pieces in the finished dish, as the fruit mashes down to thicken the sauce.

Calories: 240

450 g (1 lb) trimmed beef
1 small onion, chopped
275 g (10 oz, about 20)
  ladies' fingers (okra)
1 large banana, roughly
  chopped
1½ teaspoons sweet
  Hungarian paprika

salt
pepper
298 g (10½ oz) can ready
  to-serve consommé
1 kg (2¼ lbs) vegetable
  marrow
cress to garnish

Cut the meat into small cubes and beat with a cleaver to
tenderize. Gently heat a non-stick saucepan and drop the
cubes into the pan, a few at a time, stirring so that all sides
are sealed. Add the onion and cook, stirring frequently for
10 to 15 minutes. During this time, juice will ooze from the
meat, producing just enough gravy to prevent drying up.
Top, tail and rinse the ladies' fingers and stir them into the
meat, at the same time adding the skinned banana, the
paprika and the seasoning. As soon as the mixture regains
its heat, add the consommé. Stir thoroughly and cover
tightly with a lid. Cook over a gentle heat for about 1½
hours. From time to time inspect to make sure that the
sauce has not dried up and give the mixture a stir. After
the meat has been cooking for three-quarters of an hour,
prepare the marrow. Peel and halve it lengthwise, scoop
out the seeds, then reassemble the two halves. Wrap them
tightly in a roaster bag or foil. Place in an ovenproof dish
and bake in a fairly hot oven (190°C, 375°F, Gas 5) until
tender – about ¾ hour. To test, press the outside of the
packet. Remove from the oven, put one half of the marrow,
cut side up, back in the dish and fill the hollow with the
meat mixture, which will be nicely soft in a thick sauce.
Top with the remaining marrow half and garnish with
cress. *Serves 4.*

LEBANESE LAMB

*Leg of lamb, cut into cubes and casseroled with French beans,
tomatoes and onions enriched with red wine*

A leg of lamb weighing 1½ kg (3½ lbs) yields about 1 kg (2
lbs) of meat. After trimming, this will be reduced to about
¾ kg (1¾ lbs). Give the slimmers more beans and less meat
in this recipe. Serve with freshly cooked rice, allowing
50 g (2 oz) raw rice (about 200 calories) per non-slimmer.

Calories: 410

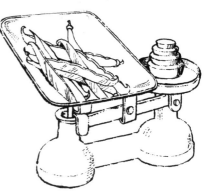

1½ kg (3½ lbs) leg of lamb
½ kg (1 lb) French beans,
    topped and tailed
227 g (8 oz) can tomatoes
2 large onions, sliced

1 clove garlic, crushed
salt
pepper
150 ml (¼ pint) red wine

Remove the meat from the bone and cut away all fat and
gristle. Cut the meat into 1 in. cubes and put in a large
shallow casserole. Cover with the beans. Empty the can of
tomatoes into a bowl, add 150 ml (¼ pint) water, mix with
the onions and garlic, and season with salt and pepper.
Pour into the casserole, cover tightly and cook in a cool
oven (160°C, 325°F, Gas 3) until the meat is tender and
can be cut through with the back of a fork. This will take
about 2 hours. After 1½ hours boil the wine in a small
saucepan until reduced by half – about 5 minutes – and
stir into the meat. If the juices seem to be drying up, add
a few tablespoons hot water. Serve on a heated platter with
a border of rice. *Serves 4 to 6.*

LEMON KEBABS

Lamb marinated in freshly made lemon tea, then skewered with fresh fruit, cucumber and tomatoes and served on a bed of lettuce and cabbage

Jackie Weller, one of my students experimenting with recipes using tea, devised these kebabs. If you enjoy lemon tea and drink it often, you can buy the leaves packeted, not in made-up powdered form which also contains sugar. Or, of course, you can make ordinary tea and flavour it with fresh lemon. Thread less banana ($\frac{1}{2}$ banana has 40 calories) and one cube of lamb less on the slimmer's skewer and hand the rice separately.

Calories: 330

300 ml ($\frac{1}{2}$ pint) freshly
   made lemon tea (using
   3 teaspoons tea leaves)
1 tablespoon vegetable oil
few sprigs fresh mint
1 tablespoon orange juice
$\frac{1}{2}$ teaspoon sugar
$\frac{1}{2}$ teaspoon salt
350 g (12 oz) trimmed
   lean lamb, cubed

1 red dessert apple
2 bananas
2 oranges
3 in. piece of cucumber
4 to 6 baby tomatoes
1 lettuce heart, shredded
$\frac{1}{4}$ white cabbage, shredded
hot cooked rice (optional)

Strain the tea into a bowl and cool. Add the oil, mint, orange juice, sugar and salt. Stir in the meat so that it is well coated. Cover and chill for 24 hours, stirring from time to time. Not more than $\frac{1}{2}$ hour before serving, prepare the fruit. Core the apple and cut into chunks. Cut the bananas into $\frac{3}{4}$ in. chunks. Peel the oranges, cut into quarters lengthways, remove any thick pith and such pips as are visible, then cut each section in half crossways. It is important to cut the oranges this way, as thin segments tend to dry up and fall to pieces under a hot grill. Slice the cucumber into twelve and remove the tomato stalks.

Remove the lamb from the marinade and thread on skewers alternately with the fruit and salad items. Preheat the grill and arrange the kebabs in the pan so that the tops just poke over the front edge. Grill the kebabs for 5 to 8 minutes until the meat is cooked. Baste frequently with the remaining marinade and turn the skewer from time to time, particularly during the first minute to seal all sides of the meat – protect your hands with oven gloves. Arrange the lettuce and cabbage on a serving dish and lay the kebabs on top, removing the skewers with the prongs of a fork at the moment of serving. *Serves 4.*

LIMBURG VEAL

A mixture of onions, garlic, green pepper, tomato, olives, mushrooms and ham, packed into veal escalopes, lined with Edam cheese, then baked with red wine

Cheese-stuffed veal escalopes baked in white wine with mushrooms, tomatoes, olives and ham at only 490 calories a portion are a must on a splurge dinner. Beat the escalopes really thinly and stuff those for the slimmers with less filling. Use luscious Dutch unsalted butter, the calories are no higher in this than in blended cheaper varieties.

Calories: 490

50 g (2 oz) unsalted butter
1 large onion, finely sliced
2 cloves garlic, crushed
1 large green pepper,
    seeded and finely sliced
4 medium tomatoes, seeded
    and chopped
12 stuffed Spanish olives
75 g (3 oz) mushrooms,
    finely sliced

50 g (2 oz) lean ham,
    finely chopped
salt
freshly ground black pepper
4 × 75 g (3 oz) slices veal
    escalope
4 × 50 g (2 oz) slices Edam
    cheese
120 ml (4 fl. oz) dry white
    wine

Heat 25 g (1 oz) of the butter, add the onion, garlic and
green pepper, and sauté for about 5 minutes, stirring
occasionally. When the vegetables are soft, but not brown,
add the tomatoes, olives, mushrooms and ham, and cook
for a further minute. Season with salt and pepper, remove
from the heat and leave to cool. Cover each veal escalope
with a cheese slice and a quarter of the filling. Fold in half
and secure with a cocktail stick. Melt the remaining butter
in a flame-proof dish or frying pan and lightly brown the
veal envelopes on each side. Transfer to an oven-proof dish
(if you have used a frying pan), pour in the wine and bake
in a fairly hot oven (190°C, 375°F, Gas 5) for 20 minutes.
Remove the cocktail sticks. Serve with creamed potato,
rice or boiled noodles, counting these extra calories of
course. *Serves 4.*

MUSHROOM AND KIDNEY RAGOÛT

*Sheep's kidneys and mushrooms in a beef and red wine sauce,
garnished with a border of mashed potato*

Ox kidney gives a good rich flavour but can be somewhat
tough. Pigs' kidney has a strong flavour. Lamb's kidney
does not produce a dark enough colour, so please use
sheep's kidney if you can get it.

Calories: 315 (including potato border)

450 g (1 lb) sheep's
  kidneys
salt
pepper
40 g (1½ oz) butter
1 small onion, finely
  chopped
25 g (1 oz) flour

300 ml (½ pint) hot beef
  stock
150 ml (¼ pint) red wine
225 g (8 oz) button
  mushrooms, sliced
225 g (8 oz) hot mashed
  potato

Wash the kidneys in cold water, then core and dry. Slice, season with salt and pepper and sauté in the butter in a non-stick pan for 5 minutes, stirring occasionally. Remove from the pan and set aside. Fry the onion briskly in the fat remaining in the pan and, when it is brown, stir in the flour. Add the stock and wine and cook, stirring all the time, until the sauce thickens. Mix in the mushrooms and kidneys, lower the heat, cover and cook gently for 10 to 15 minutes until tender. Pipe a border of mashed potato round a heated serving dish and pour the meat mixture into the centre. Serve with a green salad or mildly flavoured vegetables, such as beans, peas or carrots.   *Serves 4.*

Opposite   Moules Marinière, page 38, Danish Cucumber, page 32, Tomato Cocottes, page 44, and Apple Vichyssoise, page 27.

Overleaf   Tomato and Bacon Soup, page 43, Pork Medley, page 82, Bulgarian Sweetcorn, page 114, Poached Cucumber in Wine Sauce, page 128, plain new carrots, and Cheese and Apple Soufflé, page 140, for a hearty dinner party.

Opposite page 81   Lemon Kebabs, page 77, and Lamb and Salad Pitta, page 187.

ORANGE AND JUNIPER PORK

Four pork chops marinated in orange juice, juniper berries, garlic, Grand Marnier and ginger, then grilled and served with the juices and garnished with slices of orange and fresh mint

Pork, provided it is thoroughly trimmed of all fat, is ounce for ounce less fattening than beef or lamb similarly trimmed. Even more fat comes away when pork is grilled. Serve with plain salad and just a few potato crisps. A quarter of a small packet only costs 35 calories. If you wish to serve boiled potatoes with this recipe, offer them separately.

Calories: 235

4 × 175 g (6 oz) pork chops
2 oranges
8 juniper berries
1 clove garlic
2 teaspoons Grand Marnier
2 teaspoons Worcestershire
  sauce

few drops Tabasco pepper
  sauce
½ teaspoon ground ginger
1 teaspooon vegetable oil
fresh mint leaves

Trim the chops thoroughly. Squeeze the juice from one orange and slice the other thinly without peeling it. Crush the juniper berries and the clove of garlic with the head of a rolling pin. Prepare a marinade with orange juice, juniper, garlic, Grand Marnier, Worcestershire sauce, Tabasco pepper sauce and ginger. Add the chops and orange slices and put in the refrigerator for 4 to 6 hours, turning the chops over from time to time. Remove the chops from the marinade, brush them very lightly with oil, then grill for 5 to 6 minutes on either side. Meanwhile strain the marinade into a saucepan, reserving the fruit. Boil the liquid until reduced to 3 tablespoons. Arrange the chops on a heated dish and pour the sauce over the chops. Finally garnish with the orange slices and fresh mint. *Serves 4.*

PORK MEDLEY

Baked pork chops attractively topped with chopped egg and mustard, parsley and canned pimiento

Here's a recipe for those who like to see what they are eating and dislike dishes swimming in sauce. In this case it is the garnish that counts. Serve one parsley-sprinkled chop to the slimmer.

Calories per slimmer's portion: 140

8 × 100 g (4 oz) trimmed pork chops
salt
pepper
1 teaspoon French mustard

2 hard-boiled eggs, finely chopped
2 tablespoons chopped parsley
1 canned pimiento, drained and chopped

Grill the chops or place them on a rack in a roasting tin and bake in a fairly hot oven (200°C, 400°F, Gas 6) for 20 to 35 minutes until thoroughly cooked. Remove from the tin and pat dry with kitchen paper. Season with salt and pepper, then spread the upper surface of four of the chops with French mustard and top with egg. Spoon the chopped parsley over two chops and pile the pimiento on to the two remaining. Transfer the chops carefully to a heated long serving platter, arranging the bone ends in opposite directions and the toppings alternately as shown in the photograph. *Serves 4.*

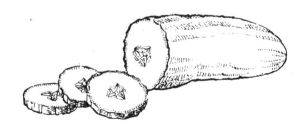

RED-COOKED BEEF WITH
CUCUMBER SHEAVES

A beautifully garnished Chinese dish of beef in a sauce of soy,
plum and tomato purée

Red cooking is a Chinese method using soy sauce and red wine. The meat is stewed very slowly to achieve maximum tenderness. It is also a simple and efficient way of producing delicious dishes with a minimum of effort.

Calories: 360–450 (depending on size of serving)

3 tablespoons plum sauce
4 tablespoons soy sauce
4 tablespoons red wine
2 tablespoons tomato purée
1 clove garlic, crushed
½ teaspoon chilli compound
   powder
1 tablespoon vegetable oil
1 medium onion, sliced into
   rings

675 g (1½ lbs) lean
   casserole beef, cut into
   1 in. cubes
salt
pepper
1 tablespoon cornflour
2 in. chunk cucumber
175 g (6 oz) French beans,
   cooked

Combine the plum and soy sauces, red wine and tomato purée and make up to 600 ml (1 pint) with boiling water. Stir in the garlic and chilli powder. Heat the oil in a large non-stick saucepan and fry the onion and the meat, (adding a few cubes at a time), stirring until well sealed and just brown. Stir in the prepared sauce, then season to taste with salt and pepper. Cover with a lid and cook gently for 3½ to 4 hours, checking now and again to make sure the liquid has not evaporated. When the meat is tender, bring to the boil and thicken with the cornflour slaked with 3 tablespoons of cold water. Without covering, stir until the sauce thickens. Keep warm while preparing the garnish. Slice the cucumber into six. Plunge slices into boiling water with the beans. As soon as the water comes back to the boil, drain thoroughly. Remove the centres of the cucumber with an apple corer or sharp knife. Slot a bunch of beans through each centre hole. Pour the meat into a heated dish and arrange three sheaves at diagonal corners. Serve at once with boiled rice or pasta.   *Serves 4 to 5.*

SPIT-ROAST PORK WITH APPLE SAUCE

Ungarnished roast pork with crispy crackling (not for the slimmer) with a separate purée of apple and lemon

The rotisserie is a particularly useful appliance for the slimmer who enjoys a roast. The surplus fat drips away as the joint is turning. Mop the roast with kitchen paper immediately after cooking. Of course the joint may also be roasted conventionally by putting the meat on a wire rack over a deep roasting tin and baking for $2\frac{1}{2}$ to $2\frac{3}{4}$ hours at 180°C, 350°F, Gas 4.

Calories: 200 (per slimmer's 2 slice portion without crackling)

$1\frac{1}{2}$ kg ($3\frac{1}{2}$ lb) joint, boned rolled loin of pork
salt
pepper
$\frac{1}{2}$ kg (1 lb) dessert apples

15 g ($\frac{1}{2}$ oz) low-calorie margarine spread
1 lemon, grated rind and juice
liquid sweetener

Preheat the rotisserie to maximum. Score the skin and season the joint, then impale and secure centrally on the spit. Fix the spit into position in the machine and roast for $1\frac{1}{2}$ hours, lowering the heat if possible after the first half-hour. To make the sauce, peel, core and slice the apples and put in a heavy-based saucepan with the margarine spread, lemon rind and juice. Add 2 tablespoons water to prevent burning, then cover and cook slowly until the apple is pulped. Press through a sieve or beat well until smooth, then sweeten to taste. Serve the sauce separately with the thinly sliced pork.   *Serves 6 to 8.*

STEAKS

Steak is often included in a slimmer's diet because it is high in protein, full of iron, filling, satisfying and, above all, easy to prepare. However, steak is very expensive and so, for a dinner party, it should be dressed up to look extravagant. Serve with a mixed salad or offer several different salads: sliced tomatoes sprinkled with fresh basil and the tiniest drop of vegetable oil; crisp Webb's lettuce torn into manageable pieces and mixed with freshly chopped chives; cucumber marinated in lemon juice and dill weed; or young chicory cut vertically into slivers. The leaner the beef, the lower the calorific value, although I must admit that meat marbled with fat is the more tasty. For your purposes, you must stick to the lean, which can be calculated at around 40 calories an ounce. I count 50 to be on the safe side. If you are entertaining a hefty man, you can hardly dish up a 100 g (4 oz) steak, and remember that meat shrinks during cooking, particularly if the heat is fierce throughout the cooking time.

STEAKS WITH GARLIC

Simple grills with garlic butter

Garlic has all sorts of magical properties and contains antiseptic and antibiotic elements – so they say. It also has a strong taste and smell which lingers on the breath. Used sparingly garlic gives savoury dishes an exotic something that need not be detectable. The garlic bulb is sometimes called a head, and a clove is a single petal. To prepare, break off a clove and peel away the crisp skin. Place the garlic between sheets of paper and flatten with a rolling pin. You can then throw away the paper and the odour at the same time. The steaks can be prepared and fried at the table if you possess an efficient fondue set. Slightly heat the pan before putting in the steaks.

Calories for slimmer's steak: 260

25 g (1 oz) salted butter	3 × 175 to 225 g (6 to 8 oz)
3 to 4 cloves garlic, crushed	lean steaks
1 tablespoon finely chopped	1 × 100 g (4 oz) lean steak
parsley	salt
1 teaspoon freshly ground	
pepper	

Blend the butter with the garlic, parsley and pepper and rub into both sides of the steaks. Fry without extra fat in a non-stick pan, sealing the steaks on both sides before completing the cooking. Season with salt and serve at once. *Serves 4.*

STEAK DE PROVENCE

Grilled steak with herbs including thyme, basil, lavender, green aniseed and savoury

I rarely recommend the use of dried herbs but, if you have to use them, make sure that they are not stale. Dried herbs have a habit of getting pushed to the back of the cupboard to languish for years. Open the container, sniff as you would for wine and, if a delectable aroma is absent, that herb will be unable to add anything to the dish. Treat yourself to one of those little pottery jars of Herbes de Provence which are a combination of thyme, basil, lavender, green aniseed and savory.

Calories for slimmer's steak: 230

3 × 175 to 225 g (6 to 8 oz)	salt
steaks	pepper
1 × 100 g (4 oz) steak	watercress to garnish
1 tablespoon vegetable oil	
2 tablespoons Herbes de	
Provence	

Brush the steaks on both sides with the oil and press into each about a half teaspoon of the herbs. Put the steaks on the grill rack and seal on both sides under a fierce pre-heated grill before lowering the heat to finish cooking. Season and garnish with watercress. *Serves 4.*

TOURNEDOS MONTPENSIER

Grilled steak with tomatoes and artichoke bottoms, flambéed with brandy

Using a pastry brush to coat the steaks makes the oil go further. Some people like to eat their steaks '*bleu*', which means that only the outside is sealed and browned, the inside remaining raw though hot. Others are put off by the sight of blood and like their steaks brown inside. When cooking for company make them all medium, when the inside meat will be pink and moist. Save the artichoke leaves for tomorrow's compensatory lunch.

Calories for slimmer's steak: 240

4 cooked globe artichokes
4 tomatoes
3×175 to 225 g (6 to 8 oz) steaks
1×100 g (4 oz) fillet steak

1 tablespoon vegetable oil
salt
pepper
2 tablespoons brandy

Pull the leaves from the artichokes and remove the hairy bases. Warm the artichoke bases between two plates set over a pan of simmering water. Skin the tomatoes, remove the tops and bottoms leaving a thick even middle slice. Brush the steaks with oil. Flash both sides under a pre-heated grill, then cook for $2\frac{1}{2}$ to $3\frac{1}{2}$ minutes on each side, putting a tomato slice on each steak for the last $\frac{1}{2}$ minute. Season with salt and pepper and stand each steak on an artichoke bottom. When serving, warm the brandy in a heatproof ladle, light with a taper and pour over the steaks. *Serves 4.*

SWEET AND SOUR LIVER

Grilled lamb's liver and cheese parcels, in a rich sauce and garnished with sliced beans

This is one of several recipes given to me by the Dutch Dairy Bureau, who recommend Edam cheese not only for its taste and versatility, but its low calorific value – 90 calories per 25 g (1 oz).

Calories: 300

450 g (1 lb) lamb's liver, thinly sliced
100 g (4 oz) Edam cheese, sliced
2 oranges
1 green pepper, seeded and finely diced
1 small onion, finely chopped

1 teaspoon soy sauce
1 teaspoon lemon juice
25 g (1 oz) brown sugar
1 teaspoon cornflour
salt
350 g (12 oz) sliced green beans, freshly cooked

Sandwich the liver with the cheese slices, secure with cocktail sticks and grill on both sides. Meanwhile squeeze the juice from 1 orange and segment the other. Put orange and juice in a saucepan with the pepper and onion and cook for 2 to 3 minutes. Add the soy sauce, lemon juice and sugar. Blend the cornflour with a few tablespoons cold water. Stir this into the sauce and cook over moderate heat, stirring constantly, until the sauce thickens. Taste and add salt if required. Remove the cocktail sticks and arrange the liver in the middle of a heated serving dish and pour the sauce over the top. Garnish with a border of the hot beans. *Serves 4.*

TONGUE WITH TOMATO AND GHERKIN SAUCE

A hot or cold dish of sliced tongue on a bed of cooked tomatoes, onions and gherkins

Ascertain that your guests will eat tongue before preparing this dish for a dinner. A small ox tongue weighs 4 lbs and would serve twelve people. Buy an unsalted tongue if you can. Cooking is fairly simple. Curl the tongue round in a large saucepan, then cover with water and bring to the boil. Change the water and simmer with a few herbs for about 5 hours until tender. Cool under cold water. Remove the skin and gristle and press the tongue under a heavy weight until cold. I cook the tomatoes in a flame-proof casserole and run less risk of the tongue breaking up, because there is no need to transfer it to a serving dish.

Calories: 300

½ kg (1 lb) firm tomatoes	1 bay leaf
salt	8 pickled pearl onions
pepper	10 small gherkins
1 tablespoon freshly chopped parsley	400 g (14 oz, 8 thin slices) cooked tongue
1 teaspoon dried basil	little grated cheese

Skin the tomatoes by immersing in boiling water for a few minutes; cut them into thin slices. Put in a heavy-based pan with salt, pepper and the herbs. Cover tightly and cook over gentle heat until soft – about 5 minutes. Add the onions whole and the gherkins cut into thin slices. Handling carefully to avoid breaking up the tongue, arrange the slices overlapping each other on the bed of vegetables. Cover and re-heat for 8–10 minutes. Serve hot or cold with a green salad or a dish of thinly sliced green-pepper circles, sprinkled with a light covering of strong grated cheese. *Serves 4.*

TON QUIN MINCE

Bowls of fried minced beef and vegetables lidded with a dry omelette

This is a fun way to serve mince, but it must be the leanest possible that you can buy. Fatty mince seems to ooze a fat that has a nasty greasy taste as well as a greasy texture. When the surplus fat is drained away, you will find that you have much less meat than you thought, so in the end it is cheapest to buy the leanest you can obtain. Alternatively, choose your own piece of meat and ask the butcher to trim it and then mince it. I always prefer to mince my own meat as it is well worth the extra effort and ensures that only the lean meat goes through the mincer. The small quantity of monosodium glutamate I have included in this recipe improves the flavour, but there is nothing to prevent you leaving it out if you prefer.

Calories: 210

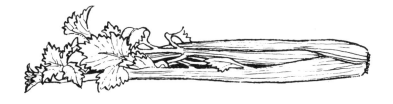

450 g (1 lb) lean, raw minced beef
1 medium onion, finely chopped
2 celery stalks, finely chopped
1 small green pepper, seeded and finely chopped

300 ml ($\frac{1}{2}$ pint) hot beef stock
397 g (14 oz) can tomatoes
2 tablespoons tomato purée
2 tablespoons soy sauce
$\frac{1}{2}$ teaspoon monosodium glutamate
salt
pepper
2 size 3 eggs

Gently heat a heavy frying pan and fry the meat without extra fat, adding a little at a time and stirring continuously with a wooden spoon. When the meat is sealed and beginning to brown, spoon away all but a tablespoon of the fat. Add the onion, celery and green pepper and fry until the vegetables soften. Pour in the stock and tomatoes. Add the tomato purée, soy sauce, monosodium glutamate and salt and pepper to taste. Lower the heat, cover with a lid and simmer gently until the meat is cooked and the sauce thick – about 30 to 40 minutes. Divide the mixture between four hot individual bowls. Keep warm. Beat the eggs with a pinch of salt and pepper and pour about a quarter of the mixture into a small non-stick frying pan. Swirl the mixture so that the surface of the pan is coated thinly. As soon as the top is set and the bottom will loosen, turn on top of one bowl of the mince. Make three more dry omelettes for the remaining servings. *Serves 4.*

TYROLEAN GOULASH

Slightly sour veal goulash in a thin tomato sauce

Use cheaper cuts of meat if you want to cut costs. Beef can be substituted for the veal but the calorific value would be higher. This is a good recipe to cook in the 'crock-pot'. The small quantity of sauce should be fairly thin since it has flour to thicken it.

Calories: 295

575 g (1¼ lbs) lean veal
4 medium onions, minced
40 g (1½ oz) butter
1 small lemon, juice and
    grated rind
1 teaspoon paprika

½ kg (1 lb) baby tomatoes,
    peeled
2 bay leaves
1 teaspoon dried oregano
1 clove garlic
salt

Cut the meat into bite-size pieces. Mix the onions, butter, lemon juice and paprika in a heavy-based saucepan and cook gently for 5 minutes. Add the meat, tomatoes, bay leaves, oregano, garlic and lemon rind. Bring to boiling point, reduce to the lowest possible heat, then add salt to taste and cover tightly. Cook gently for 3 to 3½ hours, stirring occasionally and adding a few tablespoons of water if necessary. Remove the bay leaves and garlic before serving. If you are happy to cool the dish and then reheat, you will be able to remove all the surplus butter – another way is to draw one or two pieces of starch-reduced bread over the hot surface. *Serves 4.*

VEAL ESCALOPES IN APPLE
AND SULTANA SAUCE

Grilled slices of veal coated in a fruity sauce flavoured with cloves

A 4 oz portion of veal may be rather small for a hefty masculine appetite. There should be sufficient sauce in this recipe if you wish to cook another escalope or two.

Calories: 190

25 g (1 oz) sultanas
juice of 1 orange
juice of ½ lemon
2 dessert apples
4 cloves
150 ml (¼ pint) chicken
  stock

4 × 100 g (4 oz) veal
  escalopes, flattened
salt
pepper
1 tablespoon vegetable oil

Soak the sultanas in the orange and lemon juice for 5 to 6 hours. Peel, core and chop the apples. Put the apples in a saucepan with the cloves and the stock. Cover and cook for about 20 minutes until the apples are mushy. Remove the cloves. Add the sultana mixture. Season the veal with salt and pepper and brush both surfaces with oil. Grill for 2 minutes on each side, meanwhile reheating the sauce. Arrange overlapping slices of veal on a heated serving platter and pour the sauce down the centre of the dish, leaving the edges of the meat uncoated. *Serves 4.*

VEAL LIMONE

A famous recipe adapted for the slimmer – a pot roast of veal on vegetable and lemon shreds

The Gritti Palace on the Grand Canal in Venice produces some excellent veal dishes. Among these is the original *Vitello al Limone*. Alas, it uses 75 g (3 oz) butter (678 calories). I have attempted to adapt the recipe and I am sure you will enjoy the lemony flavour contrasting with the bland meat.

Calories: 230

3 large lemons	1¼ kg (3 lb) loin of veal,
2 celery stalks	boned and rolled
2 medium carrots	150 ml (¼ pint) chicken
1 onion	stock
2 tablespoons vegetable oil	salt
	pepper

Squeeze the juice from the lemons and pare the rinds thinly so that the pitted holes are visible on the inside. Shred finely. Sliver the celery into thin strips with a potato peeler, cut the carrots into matchsticks and chop the onion. Heat the oil in a large, preferably non-stick, saucepan and brown the veal all over. Remove from the pan and set aside. Stir into the pan all the vegetables and the lemon rind. When these are well coated and just browning, replace the meat. Pour in the stock and lemon juice and season to taste. Cover with a lid and cook very gently for 2 to $2\frac{1}{2}$ hours until tender. Take out the veal, cut away the string and slice evenly. Meanwhile, boil the shredded vegetables rapidly until the liquid has nearly evaporated. Arrange the meat in overlapping slices on a heated platter and garnish with the vegetable and lemon shreds. *Serves 4.*

VEAL MARSALA

Escalopes of veal impregnated with milk, then cooked in Marsala wine

Veal fillet or escalope is very lean and is one of the lowest calorie meats. Dutch veal, if you can obtain it, is the most delicate and tender. The flesh should be creamy without any dried up brownish patches.

Calories: 225

450 g (1 lb) veal escalopes (8 slices)	5 tablespoons Marsala wine salt
150 ml ($\frac{1}{4}$ pint) skimmed milk	pepper
2 tablespoons vegetable oil	1 tablespoon freshly chopped parsley

Soak the veal in the milk for about 1 hour, turning the slices occasionally. Drain thoroughly on kitchen paper. Heat the oil in a large frying pan and brown the veal on both sides. Add the wine, salt and pepper, reduce the heat and poach the veal gently for 6 to 8 minutes, turning it over once during cooking. Arrange on a heated serving dish and sprinkle with parsley. *Serves 4.*

VEAL XEREZ

Cubes of lean veal, flambéed in brandy, then slowly casseroled with onions, mushrooms and runner beans in a sherry sauce

If you remove the alcohol from wines or spirits, only 10 per cent of the calories derived from the alcohol content will remain. So it will be of little importance, calorie-wise, whether you use dry or sweet sherry. I used medium sherry, which is also medium in the calorie scale. You will need a really large casserole for this dish.

Calories: 275

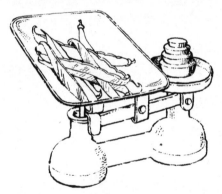

1 kg (2 lb) lean veal, cubed
salt
pepper
2 tablespoons vegetable oil
3 tablespoons brandy
3 medium onions, sliced
2 carrots, scraped and sliced
100 g (4 oz) button mushrooms

100 g (4 oz) runner beans, stringed and sliced
2 tablespoons flour
350 ml ($\frac{1}{2}$ pint) chicken stock
150 ml ($\frac{1}{4}$ pint) medium sherry
2 tablespoons tomato purée
few sprigs thyme

Season the veal with salt and pepper. Heat 1 tablespoon of the oil in a large non-stick saucepan and add the meat, a few pieces at a time, tossing until well sealed. Pour in the brandy and set alight. Transfer to a casserole when the flames have died down. Heat the remaining oil in the same saucepan. Add the vegetables, then stir briefly and clamp a lid on tightly. Shake the pan frequently while cooking over a thread of heat until the vegetables are just beginning to soften. Blend the flour with the cold stock, sherry and tomato purée, add to the vegetables then bring to the boil, stirring all the time. Lower the heat and cook for a further 5 minutes to evaporate the alcohol. Season to taste with salt and pepper. Mix in with the meat, add the sprigs of thyme, then cover the casserole and bake in a moderate oven (180°C, 350°F, Gas 4) for 1 to 1½ hours until the meat is tender. Serve from the casserole or turn on to a heated serving dish.   *Serve 6.*

4
Poultry

AUBERGINE AND TURKEY BASKETS

Aubergine shells filled with diced aubergines and turkey in a light sauce, baked and garnished with crushed crisps

Choose unblemished, unwrinkled aubergines and cut off the rough end before preparing. Salting the flesh removes the bitterness. Turkey casserole pieces are among the increasing variety of convenience foods appearing on refrigerated counters, but any uncooked turkey meat will do. Weigh after removing any bones. The crisps provide a crunchy garnish but may be omitted, saving 70 calories over all. Serve one basket as a starter, or two for a main course. Do not use turkey stock which would be too strong in this recipe.

Calories: 150

4 × 225 g (8 oz) medium
   aubergines
salt
275 g (10 oz) turkey
   casserole pieces
25 g (1 oz) butter
40 g (1½ oz) flour

300 ml (½ pint) chicken
   stock
4 tablespoons skimmed
   milk
pepper
½ small packet potato crisps
   for garnish

Halve the aubergines lengthwise, score the flesh with a sharp knife and sprinkle with salt. Leave for $\frac{1}{2}$ hour, then rinse in cold water. Scoop out the flesh using a grapefruit knife so that the shells are undamaged. Put flesh in a large saucepan of boiling water and cook for about 10 minutes until just resistant to pressure from a knife blade. Drain, then cut into small pieces. Dice the turkey and fry gently in the butter until the flesh is white on the surface. Stir in the flour, then blend in the stock and milk. Cook, stirring continuously, until the sauce thickens. Add the aubergine flesh and season with salt and pepper to taste. Divide the mixture between the aubergine shells, put into a greased, shallow ovenproof dish and bake in a moderate oven (180°C, 350°F, Gas 4) for 30 to 35 minutes until the turkey meat is tender. Crush the potato crisps and sprinkle a few over each aubergine basket just before serving.   *Serves 6.*

CHICKEN AMARILLO

Chicken breasts impregnated with oriental spices and sauced with an exquisite blend of turmeric, paprika, ginger, currants, yogurt and cream

Brown rice has a higher bran content than white rice and a delicious nutty flavour. Allow 40 g (1½ oz) raw rice per person. Rice goes a long way and is very filling. You must add the calorific value of rice to the calculations of this recipe (40 calories for a slightly rounded tablespoon of cooked rice).

Calories (excluding rice) : 310

175 g (6 oz) brown rice
4 × 175 g (6 oz) chicken breasts, skinned
15 g (½ oz) low-calorie margarine spread
1 teaspoon ground coriander
1 teaspoon salt
¼ teaspoon pepper

1 onion, finely chopped
1 tablespoon vegetable oil
1 teaspoon turmeric
1 teaspoon paprika
½ teaspoon ground ginger
120 ml (4 fl. oz) natural, low-fat yogurt
1 tablespoon currants
4 tablespoons single cream

Cook the rice in a lidded saucepan in 600 ml (1 pint) boiling salted water for about 30 to 45 minutes and, when the rice is tender, drain the surplus liquid through a colander. Rinse the rice in hot water to remove a little more of the starch. While the rice is cooking, rub the chicken with the margarine spread blended with the coriander, salt and pepper. Place in an ovenproof dish, cover and bake in a fairly hot oven (200°C, 400°F, Gas 6) for 15 minutes. Remove the lid and continue baking for a further 10 to 15 minutes until cooked. Turn off the oven, but leave the chicken inside to keep it warm while making the sauce. Sauté the onion in the oil until golden. Add the turmeric, paprika and ginger and cook gently for 1 minute before stirring in the yogurt, currants and cream. Heat the sauce carefully without allowing it to boil. Coat the chicken with the sauce and serve on a bed of rice. *Serves 4.*

CHICKEN CHAMPAGNE

Chicken joints cooked with fresh orange and lemon juices,
Champagne, mushrooms, brandy and cream

Choose a medium Champagne for a sweeter flavour or substitute a sparkling wine such as Asti Spumante, Garcia or one of the sweet Spanish sparkling wines. Champagne only comes from one area of France, so that all other wine-growers must call their wines by another name, although quite a number make their wine in a similar manner to that used in Champagne. The calories in this and the brandy are mostly in the alcohol. The wine accounts for only 120 calories, but only one-third is lost in cooking since the casserole is covered during the cooking period.

Calories: 400

50 g (2 oz) butter
4 × 250 g (9 oz) chicken
    joints
1 large onion, sliced
2 tablespoons flour
1 tablespoon tomato purée
1 tablespoon fresh lemon
    juice
4 tablespoons fresh orange
    juice
2 teaspoons finely grated
    orange zest

$\frac{1}{4}$ teaspoon grated mace
175 ml (6 fl. oz, quarter
    bottle) Champagne
225 g (8 oz) button
    mushrooms, sliced
salt
pepper
2 tablespoons single
    cream
3 tablespoons brandy

Heat the butter in a large saucepan and brown the chicken on both sides. Transfer to an ovenproof casserole. Fry the onion in the remaining fat, then stir in the flour, tomato purée, fruit juices, grated zest and mace. Cook until bubbling, stirring all the time. Thin down with the Champagne, stir in the mushrooms and season to taste with salt and pepper. Pour the sauce over the chicken, put the lid on tightly and bake in a moderate oven (180°C, 350°C, Gas

4) for 1 to 1¼ hours until the chicken is tender. Stir in the cream. Arrange the chicken on a heated serving dish. Warm the brandy in a metal ladle, ignite and pour over the chicken when serving. *Serves 4.*

CHICKEN GOULYAS

Sweet Hungarian paprika and bay leaves are gently cooked with the chicken until it is soft – soured cream adds a final touch

The paprika is the overriding flavour in a goulyas, so it should be carefully selected. Try to buy a sweet variety, which I think goes well with chicken.

Calories: 285

4 × 250 g (9 oz) chicken joints, skinned	1 clove garlic, crushed
salt	2 tablespoons flour
pepper	396 g (14 oz) can tomatoes
2 tablespoons vegetable oil	1 tablespoon paprika
1 medium onion, sliced	4 bay leaves
	7 tablespoons soured cream

Season the chicken with salt and pepper and fry lightly in the hot oil. Remove from the pan and drain. Fry the onion and garlic in the remaining oil until soft. Stir in the flour. As soon as it is blended, add the tomatoes, paprika, bay leaves and just over 300 ml (½ pint) water. Bring to the boil, stirring gently all the time. Add salt and pepper to taste. Put in the chicken, reduce the heat and cover with a lid. Cook very gently for 1¼ to 1½ hours until the chicken is soft, but not so soft that it falls apart. Check the amount of liquid from time to time, adding more water if necessary to the consistency of unwhipped double cream. Lift out the chicken, remove the bones, then replace in the saucepan and stir in the soured cream. Reheat but do not boil. Remember to take out the bay leaves before serving. *Serves 4.*

CHICKEN IN ORANGE SAUCE

Pan-fried chicken baked in a cool oven with orange juice and crispy bacon bits

The bacon slicer was evident in every grocer's shop in bygone days when customers could have any thickness they wanted. The thickness was indicated by numbers – the highest indicated the thickest, so number 2 slices would be wafer thin. Alas, in most shops now you are served with number 6 and much of the bacon is pre-packed. It is very difficult to calculate exact calorific values for bacon, as some is fattier than others. In this recipe I am reckoning on twenty rashers to the pound.

Calories: 470

4 rashers streaky bacon
1 tablespoon vegetable oil
1½ kg (3½ lb) chicken,
　skinned and cut into 8
　pieces
salt
pepper
8 baby tomatoes
1 onion, sliced

4 tablespoons flour
1 chicken stock cube
　(optional)
600 ml (1 pint) fresh
　orange juice (or
　equivalent reconstituted)
1 orange, thinly sliced
few sprigs parsley

Remove the rinds, and bone and slice the bacon into narrow strips. Fry in the oil until crispy. Remove with a slotted spoon. Dry the chicken pieces, season with salt and pepper and brown in the same fat. Drain and arrange in an attractive casserole with the tomatoes. Now put the onion in the pan and fry until soft but not brown. Stir in the flour, stock cube, orange juice and bacon. Bring to the boil, stirring all the time. As soon as the sauce thickens, pour it over the chicken, cover with a lid and bake in a cool oven (160°C, 325°F, Gas 3) for ¾ to 1 hour until the chicken is tender. Garnish with overlapping slices of orange and place a few sprigs of parsley wherever there is a gap. *Serves 4.*

CHICKEN PETROUCHKA

*Chicken pieces in their own rich stock liberally sauced with
tomato ketchup and garnished with chopped walnuts*

Make sure all poultry is fully thawed before cooking. You
are meant to keep the bones in the chicken in this recipe to
give the dish a rich, home-made flavour. You don't need
any guidance if you choose chicken pieces but, if you buy a
whole chicken, remember to take the giblets out and wash
the cavity with cold water and a little salt before chopping.
Then put the chicken on a wooden board – it will slip on a
laminated one. Take the heftiest knife you have, insert it
through the cavity and hit the handle of the knife with the
head of a wooden rolling pin or a hammer. Take out the
knife, put it in the other end and repeat. You can then open
out the chicken. Turn it over and repeat the process. The
rest of the chopping should be relatively easy.

Calories: 310–460 (depending on size of serving)

1 tablespoon vegetable oil
1½ kg (3½ lb) oven-ready
   chicken, chopped into
   small pieces
4 medium onions, finely
   sliced
1 clove garlic, crushed

150 ml (5 fl. oz) tomato
   ketchup
1 teaspoon paprika
salt
pepper
6 walnut halves, chopped

Heat the oil. Add the chicken and toss until brown. Add
the onion and garlic, cover with a lid and cook gently until
the onion is soft – about 4 minutes. Shake the pan occasionally to avoid sticking. Stir in the ketchup, paprika and
300 ml (½ pint) water, bring to the boil, then season to
taste with salt and pepper. Lower the heat, cover and
simmer for 30 minutes until the chicken is tender and the
sauce pleasantly thick. Check from time to time, adding
water if necessary. Turn on to a heated serving dish and
sprinkle with chopped walnuts. *Serves 4 to 6.*

CHICKEN SUPRÈMES IN SPICED MAYONNAISE

Delicate cold breast of chicken coated in a mayonnaise spiced with sieved apple, onion and curry powder

No one will suspect that this is a low-calorie dish. It is a bit fiddly to prepare so you may as well make a double quantity while you are about it. If you wish to halve the recipe, on the other hand, be sure to make the mayonnaise in the narrowest possible jug or bowl so that the mixer beaters only just clear the sides. Serve this dish with both an oriental and a green salad.

Calories: 370 per portion

8 × 100 g (4 oz) boned chicken breasts, skinned
salt
pepper
1 small onion, minced
½ dessert apple, chopped
1 tablespoon curry powder
2 eggs, separated
½ teaspoon dry mustard powder
¼ teaspoon salt
¼ teaspoon pepper
9 tablespoons olive oil, at room temperature
2 teaspoons white vinegar
3 tablespoons natural, low-fat yogurt
paprika

Season the chicken with salt and pepper. Put in a large frying pan, barely cover with water, put on a lid and poach until tender. Remove the suprèmes with a slotted spoon and drain thoroughly. Cool. Boil down the stock remaining in the pan until about a cup is left. Add the onion, apple and curry powder and cook until pulpy and nearly dry. If any small pieces remain, press through a sieve, but this is not strictly necessary. Leave until cold. Beat the egg yolks, mustard, salt and pepper until creamy. Whisk in the oil, drop by drop, until a thick mayonnaise is formed. Stir in the vinegar, then whisk in the remaining oil, pouring this in a steady trickle. When all the oil is incorporated, stir in the yogurt and curry pulp. Whisk the egg whites with clean grease-free beaters until peaks form. Fold into the mayonnaise. Arrange the suprèmes on a chilled platter. Stainless steel lends itself very well to this. Coat with the sauce and sprinkle a thin line of paprika on each piece. *Serves 8.*

DUCK À L'ORANGE

Roast duck with a separate sauce of orange rind and juice, Vermouth and a touch of sugar

Duck is fattier and has 40 more calories to the ounce than chicken, but it is a favourite party dish. You could use wild duck in this recipe, when the calorie value would be similar to that of chicken. Serve yourself with lean breast only and leave the skin on the plate.

Calories (4 oz slimmer's portion) : 390

1½ kg (3½ lb) oven-ready duck	1 teaspoon sugar
	salt
1 large orange	pepper
150 ml (¼ pint) orange juice	1 teaspoon cornflour
	watercress to garnish
150 ml (¼ pint) dry white Vermouth	

Place the duck in a dry roasting tin and cook in a moderate oven (180°C, 350°F, Gas 4) for 1½ to 1¾ hours until the juices run clear when the thigh is pierced with a fork. Spoon away any fat that may have accumulated. While the duck is cooking, pare the rind from the orange, put the rind into cold water and boil for 10 minutes to remove the bitterness. Drain and cut into thin strips. Cut away all the white pith from the orange and slice into rings. Put into a saucepan with the strips of rind, the orange juice and Vermouth and bring to the boil. Stir in the sugar and add salt and pepper to taste. Blend the cornflour with a tablespoon of cold water, stir this into the sauce and bring back to the boil. Serve the duck on a carving dish, garnish with the orange rings and watercress and serve the sauce separately.   *Serves 4.*

HOMESTEAD CHICKEN

As the name suggests this is a chicken casserole with a mixture of vegetables of your choice

Prepare all the vegetables in advance and this dish can be put together in no time at all. Vary the vegetables if you like but make sure that the slow-cooking types, for example celery and swede, are cut into small pieces. Use a deep flameproof casserole to reduce the washing-up.

Calories: 195–235 (depending on size of serving)

4 × 250 g (9 oz) fresh
    chicken joints, skinned
    and halved
25 g (1 oz) butter
1 medium onion, chopped
4 celery stalks, sliced
2 carrots, sliced into rings
1 small swede, peeled and
    diced
1 medium leek, sliced

8 medium Brussels sprouts
227 g (8 oz) can tomatoes
300 ml (½ pint) chicken
    stock
2 bay leaves
1 tablespoon chopped
    parsley
salt
pepper
pinch sugar

Fry the chicken gently in the butter until brown – about 10 minutes. Remove from the casserole and fry the onion and celery in it. Replace the chicken and all the remaining ingredients. Cover with a lid, transfer to a cool oven (160°C, 325°F, Gas 3) and cook for 1¼ to 1½ hours until both the chicken and vegetables are tender. After the chicken has been cooking for 1 hour, remove the lid, taste and adjust the seasoning. Leave the casserole uncovered for the remaining cooking time if there is an excess of liquid. Remove the bay leaves before serving. *Serves 5 to 6.*

HONEYED CHICKEN

Grilled chicken glazed with clear honey and orange and garnished with watercress

Here is another recipe that can be simplified or cut down to serve one person. If you are serving this for company, make sure that the dish is garnished exquisitely. Enjoyment of food is 90 per cent in the eye of the beholder. When you are on your own, substitute any unsweetened canned orange juice you may have in the refrigerator for the fresh orange juice. 6 tablespoons canned juice equals one small orange (30 calories).

Calories: 290

4 × 250 g (9 oz) chicken
   joints, skinned
1 tablespoon vegetable oil
salt

pepper
3 small oranges
3 level tablespoons clear
   honey

Garnish
1 orange, sliced thinly with one incision from centre to edge
few sprigs watercress

Brush the chicken with oil and season with salt and pepper. Remove the rack from the grill pan, put in the chicken and cook under a medium heat for about 25 to 30 minutes until tender. Turn the chicken pieces over at least once during cooking and baste with any juices that collect in the pan. Squeeze the juice from the oranges and mix it with the honey. Drain the excess fat from the grill pan, pour the orange mixture over the chicken and grill for a further 5 minutes to set the glaze. Arrange the chicken joints on a heated dish and garnish with orange slices twisted and sprigs of watercress.   *Serves 4.*

PHEASANT AUBERGE

Casseroled pheasant with onion, apple and cider sauce

Pheasant is usually browned in butter before casseroling, but the flavour is not impaired if you omit browning from this recipe.

Calories: 450–525 (depending on size of serving)

2×1 kg ($2\frac{1}{4}$ lb) pheasants, dressed weight
salt
pepper

1 large cooking apple, peeled and sliced
1 onion, sliced
200 ml ($7\frac{1}{2}$ fl. oz) dry cider
1 tablespoon cornflour

Cut the pheasants into quarters. Season with salt and pepper and arrange in a greased casserole, skin side down. Cover with the apple and onion slices and pour the cider over. Cover tightly and cook in a moderate oven (180°C,

350°F, Gas 4) for $\frac{3}{4}$ to 1 hour until tender. Lift the pheasant pieces on to a heated serving dish. Blend the cornflour with 1 or 2 tablespoons cold water. Strain the pheasant juices into a saucepan, add the slaked cornflour and bring to the boil, stirring continuously until the sauce thickens. Pour the sauce over the pheasant and serve immediately. *Serves 6 to 7.*

POLLO ALLA CATALANA

Slices of shiny red peppers, tomatoes and sherry mixed with small pieces of fried chicken and cooked in a pan on top of the stove

The chicken is not immersed in a thick sauce but comfortably bedded in thick red-coloured vegetables. The flavour is mild and sweet and is derived from the gloriously ripe red peppers.

Calories: 385

$1\frac{1}{4}$ kg ($2\frac{1}{2}$ lb) chicken
3 tablespoons vegetable oil
salt
pepper
3 tablespoons medium
   sherry

1 onion, finely chopped
1 clove garlic, crushed
1 large red pepper, seeded
   and sliced
227 g (8 oz) can tomatoes

Remove as much of the skin as possible from the chicken and cut into eight. Fry in the oil until golden brown. Remove from the pan, season with salt and pepper and sprinkle with the sherry. In the same pan fry the onion, garlic and pepper gently until softening – about 5 minutes. Add the tomatoes, replace the chicken, then cover and cook until tender – about 25 minutes. Taste and adjust the seasoning 10 minutes before the end of cooking, adding a few tablespoons of boiling water to moisten if necessary. *Serves 4.*

PRAWN AND TURKEY CHOW MEIN

Cooked turkey, peeled prawns and bean sprouts with red and green peppers in a mushroom, sherry and soy sauce

Chow mein is a traditional Chinese description for a dish with fried noodle topping. Chop suey is an American invention of mixed chopped ingredients cooked with soy sauce. Serve this recipe with boiled noodles, 30 calories to the ounce when cooked.

Calories: 250

1 tablespoon vegetable oil
1 small onion, chopped
2 celery stalks, chopped
2 rounded tablespoons diced green peppers
2 rounded tablespoons diced red peppers
156 g (5½ oz) can condensed cream of mushroom soup

1 tablespoon soy sauce
2 tablespoons medium sherry
salt
pepper
225 g (8 oz) cooked turkey, diced
100 g (4 oz) peeled prawns
175 g (6 oz) bean sprouts, rinsed and drained

Heat the oil and sauté the onion, celery and peppers for 3 to 4 minutes. When slightly softened but by no means cooked, stir in the soup, soy sauce and sherry. Season to taste with salt and pepper, then add the turkey and prawns. Bring to steaming, but not quite boiling point. Quickly mix in the bean sprouts and serve at once.   *Serves 4.*

SALT-BAKED CHICKEN

Roast chicken encased in sea salt

Contrary to popular belief, poultry roasted when encased in salt does not make the flesh taste too salty. Provided the skin is unbroken, the salt remains on the outside and forms a wall to keep in all the flavour. The flesh should be moist and succulent. Horseradish sauce (10 calories per tablespoon) gives a delightful contrasting flavour but should be served separately.

Calories: 320 (including the crispy skin)

1¼ kg (2½ lb) ready-to-cook chicken
50 g (2 oz) butter, softened

50 g (2 oz) low-fat soft cheese (Jockey or Speisequark)
2 handfuls coarse sea salt

Prepare a very hot oven (230°C, 450°F, Gas 8). Make sure the chicken is dry. Rub the butter into the skin, working it well in and spread the cheese inside the cavity. Press a crust of salt all over the chicken, place breast side down in a roasting tin and cook for about three-quarters of an hour, basting twice during the last 10 minutes. When the chicken is ready it should be golden, crusty, smooth and inflated. Serve at once, removing the skin at the table.   *Serves 4.*

TROPICAL CHICKEN

Chicken joints encircling a pile of freshly grilled fruit and nuts, garnished with milky cheese

Fruit sauces without added sugar are low in calories. I serve this as a summer supper dish, starting with a cold soup such as iced cucumber or vichyssoise followed with chocolate meringue or pancake cigars (page 149).

Calories: 300

4 × 250 g (9 oz) chicken
  joints, skinned
salt
pepper
1 tablespoon vegetable oil
1 large orange
6 white grapes, seeded and
  skinned

3 black grapes, seeded and
  skinned
1 banana, sliced
4 in. wedge watermelon
15 g ($\frac{1}{2}$ oz) slivered
  almonds, toasted
2 tablespoons skimmed-
  milk soft cheese

Season the chicken with salt and pepper and brush with oil. Remove the rack and grill the chicken in the base of the pan until golden brown on each side – about 10 minutes. Switch off heat and leave in the pan. While the chicken is cooking prepare the fruit. Segment the orange, removing all the membranes. Put the flesh into a bowl and chop to allow the juice to come out. Add the grapes, the banana and the watermelon, seeded and cut into $\frac{1}{2}$ in. dice. Transfer the chicken to a heated round serving dish, making a well in the middle. Put all the fruit and nuts into the grill pan and heat rapidly for 2 or 3 minutes. Stir in the cheese and pile the mixture into the centre of the chicken. *Serves 4.*

5
Vegetables & Salads

BROCCOLI SALAD

Chilled cooked broccoli sauced with tomato purée, soft cheese and chopped hard-boiled eggs

Salads are usually served individually, making sly cutting down easy. Here is one that goes a long way, looks a lot and could make a low-calorie meal in itself. I used a 'Jockey' cheese (35 calories per ounce or 28·5 g) but you can use any of the runny white cheeses. Calorific value is usually printed on the packet.

Calories: 100

½ kg (1 lb) tight-headed broccoli
1 tablespoon tomato purée
100 g (4 oz) low-fat soft cheese (Jockey)
2 hard-boiled eggs, size 3 or 4, finely chopped
salt
pepper
1 tablespoon freshly chopped parsley

Trim any leaves and tough stalk from the broccoli. Wash in cold water, then simmer in a covered pan of lightly salted water until just tender – about 15 minutes. Drain carefully and leave to cool, then arrange in a shallow dish. Beat the tomato purée into the cheese, then combine with the eggs and season to taste. Pour over the broccoli and sprinkle with parsley. Cover with cling film and chill for 2 hours before serving. *Serves 4.*

BULGARIAN SWEETCORN

Onion-flavoured kernels mixed with yogurt

I prefer to scrape the kernels from fresh corn cobs (you need three cobs for this recipe), but frozen or canned sweetcorn will do as well.

Calories: 105

1 small onion
15 g ($\frac{1}{2}$ oz) unsalted butter
225 g (8 oz) sweetcorn
   kernels, cooked

150 ml ($\frac{1}{4}$ pint) natural,
   low-fat yogurt
salt
pepper

Finely chop the onion and sauté in the butter until soft. Drain and wipe the excess fat from the pan with thickly folded kitchen paper. Mix all the ingredients together and reheat very gently. The mixture must not boil or the yogurt may curdle.   *Serves 4.*

CARROT MINT SALAD

Grated carrot with fresh mint and yogurt dressing

Herbs and spices, frequently added to vegetarian dishes, are also effective in slimming diets. They replace the flavour which is inevitably lost when so little fat may be used. One of the problems with herbs is that the dried kind are only flavoursome when used in cooked dishes, and few fresh varieties are available. Mint grows like wildfire, to the regret of serious gardeners, so it is easy to get hold of. I am the world's worst gardener, but even I have successfully propagated (if that's the right word) mint in a pot in the garden. Any surplus to your requirements can be simply frozen. Wash and dry the mint, remove the tougher stems, then put it in a polythene bag, seal and freeze. When you want to use it, you will be able to remove a few of the leaves and crush them easily in the hand. This salad should be eaten freshly prepared or within one day of preparation.

Calories: 25

350 g (12 oz, 5 or 6) firm carrots
4 to 6 leaves fresh mint

5 tablespoons natural, low-fat yogurt
salt
pepper

Grate the carrots, finely chop the mint and mix with the yogurt. Add salt and pepper to taste. Cover and store in the refrigerator until required. *Serves 4.*

CAULIFLOWER FLORETTES ROMAGNA

Cooked cauliflower sprigs garnished with fried onion, marjoram and Parma ham

Save the stalks and leaves to use in soups or make a vegetable stock. When vegetables are boiled the vitamins escape into the water, which also absorbs some of the flavour, so don't throw the valuable liquid away. Sometimes I use the cooking water from boiled potatoes for boiling carrots and then for sprouts, topping it up with more clear water if necessary. Finally I use it to make soup.

Calories: 85

1 medium to large
    cauliflower
salt
15 g ($\frac{1}{2}$ oz) butter
1 small onion, finely
    chopped

1 teaspoon chopped
    marjoram
1 thin slice Parma ham,
    diced

Remove the outer leaves and stalks from the cauliflower and break the head into even-sized florettes. Simmer these in salted water in a lidded saucepan for 10 to 15 minutes until not quite tender. Switch off the heat but leave the florettes in the saucepan to keep hot while preparing the topping. Heat the butter and fry the onion until just brown. Stir in the marjoram and the ham and cook for $\frac{1}{2}$ minute. Drain the cauliflower and pile into a round heated serving dish, flower part upwards. Drain away the surplus butter and sprinkle onion mixture on top. Serve at once. *Serves 4.*

CELERIAC WITH PARSLEY SAUCE

White-sauced celeriac cubes

Celeriac tastes like celery and looks like a swede. It is wonderful as a salad, finely grated, seasoned and dressed with a modicum of lemon juice and oil. It is also an entirely acceptable cooked vegetable.

Calories: 50

450 g (1 lb) celeriac
750 ml (1$\frac{1}{4}$ pint) well-
    flavoured chicken stock
1 tablespoon cornflour
2 tablespoons skimmed
    milk

1 tablespoon freshly
    chopped parsley
salt
pepper
1 teaspoon butter

Scrub and peel the celeriac and cut into small pieces. Simmer in the chicken stock for 40 to 50 minutes until tender. Strain into a bowl. Blend the cornflour with the milk, add 300 ml ($\frac{1}{2}$ pint) of the strained liquid and return it to the saucepan. Bring to the boil, stirring continuously until the sauce thickens, then add the parsley. Cook for a further $\frac{1}{2}$ minute. Adjust the seasoning and stir in the butter. Put the celeriac in a heated serving dish and pour the sauce over it. *Serves 4.*

CELERY ORCHARD SALAD

Combination of celery, oranges, dessert apples and lemon juice, sprinkled with hazel nuts

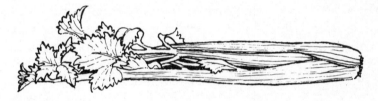

Slimmers rely considerably on salads because these provide a large amount to eat, yet have a low calorific value. Don't think only in terms of lettuce and tomato, for there are many combinations that are both exciting and delicious. While you are chopping and grating, you might as well make a fair amount and grating gives a considerable illusion of quantity. Remember some salads store better than others. This one will keep in the refrigerator for a few days, improving its flavour after 24 hours. The salad is as refreshing as a spring morning and can be served as a lunch on its own or with the usual green salad.

Calories : 70

1 bunch celery	squeeze fresh lemon juice
2 juicy oranges	2 tablespoons grated
1 green dessert apple	roasted hazelnuts

Trim the celery stalks and slice finely. Peel the orange, cut across in half and remove any pips. Chop the flesh (there is no need to remove the membranes). Wash the apple, core and quarter it, then slice finely without peeling. Mix the fruit and celery together, add the lemon juice, arrange in a dish and sprinkle with the hazelnuts. Cover and refrigerate for at least 12 hours. *Serves 4.*

CHINESE TOSSED CABBAGE

Sautéed shredded cabbage and onion in ground ginger and soy sauce

A non-stick saucepan makes it possible to sauté in negligible quantities of fat. Our family like vegetables crisp and not stewed to death, because they are used to the microwave oven, which is so marvellous for cooking vegetables without beating them to a pulp. If you prefer your vegetables a little softer, just cook when covered for a little longer. Reheat in the saucepan over medium heat.

Calories: 70

$\frac{1}{2}$ kg (1 lb, 1 medium) firm white cabbage	salt
	pepper
1 small onion	$\frac{1}{4}$ teaspoon ground ginger
1 tablespoon vegetable oil	1 tablespoon soy sauce

Shred the cabbage and chop the onion finely. Heat the oil in a deep non-stick saucepan, add the onion and sauté, stirring constantly with a wooden spoon until the onion is soft but not browned. Toss in the cabbage and, keeping the heat fairly high, stir vigorously for about 3 minutes, turning the cabbage shreds so that all have touched the saucepan base. As soon as the cabbage begins to change colour, add the salt, pepper, ground ginger and then the soy sauce. Lower the heat and cook for one more minute. Immediately turn into a lidded dish. *Serves 4.*

CONCHITA'S HOT BEANS

Runner beans, tomato purée and fresh chilli in thickened sauce

Whenever cooking in a lidded pan, make sure the heat is low or the lid will lift off and frothy liquid pour down in a Niagara Falls fashion. Another problem with the lidded pan is that liquid can dry up even when you feel quite sure it won't. Have a look occasionally and add more water if this seems to be sensible, unless you are a particularly dab-hand with burnt pans.

Calories: 30

½ kg (1 lb) young runner beans
2 tablespoons tomato purée
1 teaspoon salt
pinch ground cinnamon

1 fresh green chilli
2 teaspoons cornflour
1 tablespoon freshly chopped parsley

Top and tail the beans and remove the strings from the sides. Cut into ⅛ in. slices and put in a heavy-based sauce-pan with the tomato purée, salt, cinnamon and 300 ml (½ pint) water. Put the chilli into a small pan, adding sufficient cold water to cover. Bring to the boil and simmer for 5 minutes. Lift the chilli out with a slotted spoon on to a board and slice paper thin with a knife and fork (some people find that chillis irritate the skin). Add to the beans, then cover and cook gently for about 30 minutes, stirring occasionally, until the beans are nearly tender. Blend the cornflour with 2 or 3 tablespoons cold water. Stir it into the beans and, without covering, cook gently for 5 to 10 minutes until the beans are nicely coated in a smooth sauce. Turn into a heated serving dish and sprinkle with chopped parsley. *Serves 4.*

COURGETTES AND LETTUCE SAUTÉ

Grated courgettes and lettuce cooked with onion and nutmeg

Cook '*al dente*' – that is the Italian way of saying that food should be cooked tenderly enough for the teeth to close through it with little resistance. Don't cook something until it is so soft that you can mash it with the tongue against the roof of the mouth.

Calories: 55

½ kg (1 lb, 7 medium)
  courgettes
salt
1 very small onion
6 or 8 outer leaves of a cos
  lettuce

1 tablespoon vegetable
  oil
½ teaspoon ground nutmeg
¼ teaspoon pepper

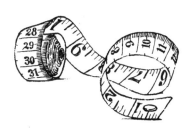

Top and tail the courgettes, but do not peel. Grate finely, put on a plate, sprinkle with salt and leave for half an hour. Chop the onion, remove the thick stems of the lettuce and cut it in ½ in. slices. Sauté the onion in the oil in a non-stick saucepan until soft. Stir in the nutmeg and a generous shake of pepper. Add the lettuce, tossing until it is well coated and the colour just deepening. Drain the courgettes and squeeze out any remaining juices by hand. Add them to the lettuce and cook over a thread of heat until only just tender. Add salt to taste. Switch off the heat, cover with a lid and leave for a few minutes before serving. *Serves 4.*

COURGETTES MARINATA

Courgettes impregnated with herbs and cooked in the resulting marinade

The courgettes are mixed with herbs and left for several hours in this recipe before being cooked. This enables the flavours of the herbs to penetrate the vegetable fully – much more effective if you can use fresh or frozen herbs rather than the dry variety. You will need to stay in the kitchen while cooking the courgettes – if they dry out, you will find a sticky gunge in the bottom of the pan.

Calories: 85

½ kg (1 lb) even-sized courgettes
1 bay leaf, crushed
1 tablespoon freshly chopped parsley
1 teaspoon tarragon leaves
½ teaspoon thyme leaves
½ teaspoon salt

¼ teaspoon freshly ground white pepper
1 small clove garlic, crushed
1 tablespoon fresh lemon juice
2 tablespoons vegetable oil

Top and tail the courgettes and cut them into ½ in. slices. Put in a ceramic or glass bowl with all the other ingredients, cover and leave for several hours in a cool place, stirring once or twice. Transfer to a non-stick saucepan, add 2 or 3 tablespoons water, cover and cook gently for 12 to 15 minutes, shaking the pan from time to time. *Serves 4.*

CREAMED CHICORY

Cooked chicory leaves garnished with cream and cress

In Belgium chicory is called endive, in Britain endive is a curly green salad vegetable and chicory is a white-leafed bulb. So, Common Market or no, this recipe is for the latter.

Raw chicory can taste bitter, but when cooked it has a milder flavour.

Calories: 85

450 g (1 lb) chicory (8 small heads)	salt
15 g ($\frac{1}{2}$ oz) butter	pepper
2 teaspoons fresh lemon juice	4 tablespoons single cream
	cress to garnish

Trim the ends of the chicory and wash it. Put into a saucepan with the butter, lemon juice and salt to taste. Bring to the boil, then lower the heat, cover with a lid and simmer for 30 to 40 minutes until it is tender and most of the liquid has evaporated. Drain and return the chicory to the saucepan but do not reheat. Add a shake of pepper, stir in the cream, then turn into a heated serving dish and sprinkle with cress. *Serves 4.*

DUCHESSE POTATOES

Whirls of piped potato browned in the oven

Duchesse potatoes – pyramids or nests of creamed potatoes – look good as a garnish and go further because they are piped which gives a greater volume. They may be prepared in advance and baked when required. Serve only one pyramid to the slimmer.

Calories: 65 (for 1 pyramid)

675 g (1$\frac{1}{2}$ lbs) potatoes, peeled	2 tablespoons skimmed milk
40 g (1$\frac{1}{2}$ oz) low-calorie margarine spread	1 size 3 egg, beaten
	salt
	pepper

Preheat a fairly hot oven (190°C, 375°F, Gas 5). Boil the potatoes until soft – about 20 minutes. Drain, then return them to the saucepan and stir over the lowest heat to dry. Press through a sieve, then beat in the margarine spread, 1 tablespoon milk and about three-quarters of the egg. Season with salt and pepper to taste. Check that the mixture is soft enough to pipe, then put into a large piping bag fitted with a $\frac{1}{2}$ in. star nozzle. Pipe twelve potato pyramids on to a baking sheet lined with non-stick paper. Blend the remaining milk and egg together and brush over the potatoes. Bake for about 20 to 30 minutes until golden brown but not over-crisp. *Serves 6.*

GARDENER'S SALAD

Thinly sliced combination salad comprising button mushrooms, carrots, onion, green pepper, tomatoes and orange

An unlikely combination at first sight, but the orange imparts its acidic properties to the onion, making it bland and the mushrooms and carrots more tender. The salad requires no additional dressing.

Calories : 50

100 g (4 oz) button mushrooms	1 green pepper
225 g ($\frac{1}{2}$ lb) carrots	2 tomatoes
1 small onion	1 large orange

Prepare the vegetables in the usual way, cutting them into manageable pieces. Pare away the orange skin so that the flesh is showing, then cut into quarters. Slice all the ingredients thinly, preferably using a food processor. Mix thoroughly, then cover and leave in a cool place for at least 12 hours before serving. *Serves 4.*

LETTUCE AND WALNUT SALAD

Crisp lettuce heart and walnuts tossed in yogurt, lemon juice, mustard and parsley

Fresh walnuts taste marvellous but they are not always available. Packets of walnut halves, sold in most grocers shops, must be in good condition when purchased. Shelled walnuts go rancid more quickly than any other variety of nut and are therefore better stored in the freezer. They also tend to be bitter, but you can regenerate them by putting them in a saucepan, covering with water, bringing to the boil and draining. Repeat this twice, then cover the drained nuts with cold water and refrigerate for 24 hours. The only disadvantage is that they will have become so moist and delicious that you will have to be well disciplined to keep from nibbling them. This recipe is a great appetite depressant when served as a starter.

Calories: 80

4 tablespoons natural, low-fat yogurt
1 teaspoon fresh lemon juice
pinch salt
pinch (no more) sugar
1 teaspoon Dijon mustard

3 crisp, round lettuce hearts
24 fresh or soaked walnut halves
2 tablespoons freshly chopped parsley

Combine the yogurt, lemon juice, salt, sugar and mustard in a large bowl. Shred the lettuce and chop the walnuts. Just before serving add the lettuce and walnuts to the dressing and toss thoroughly. Put into individual wooden bowls and garnish with the parsley. *Serves 4.*

MARROW LOMBARDIA

Sliced marrow coated with a bacon, onion and tomato sauce

Marrow isn't to everybody's taste but its calorific value is negligible, which might persuade those who don't like it to have a go. The sauce does wonders for this vegetable.

Calories: 45

1¼ kg (2½ lb) marrow
salt
1 rasher streaky bacon
1 small onion, finely
   chopped

396 g (14 oz) can tomatoes,
   drained
2 tablespoons tomato
   purée
pepper

Peel the marrow, cut in half lengthwise and scoop out the seeds. Cut the flesh into ½ in. slices. Simmer in salted water until just tender. Meanwhile fry the bacon very gently in its own fat in a non-stick pan. Remove it from the pan and cut away the rind. Bone and chop. Fry the onion in the remaining fat. Drain. Rub the tomatoes through a sieve. Combine the pulped tomatoes, bacon, onion, tomato purée, salt and pepper and poach gently in a lidded pan for 20 to 25 minutes. Drain the marrow and arrange in overlapping slices on a heated dish. Pour on the sauce. *Serves 4.*

OKRA AND TOMATO HOTPOT

A vegetable casserole crumbed and browned under the grill

Stick to your favourite brand of tomatoes and don't be tempted to try cheaper cans. I have found some to contain much more juice than tomatoes and even the juice is sometimes very thin. Drain the tomatoes for this recipe, but keep the juice for drinking, zipped up with a dash of Lea and Perrin's Worcestershire sauce and a pinch of salt (30 calories per teacupful).

Calories: 80

24 okra (ladies' fingers)	sea salt
1 onion	black peppercorns, freshly
396 g (14 oz) can tomatoes	ground
5 tablespoons dried	25 g (1 oz) low-calorie
breadcrumbs	margarine spread

Wash the okra in cold water, then top and tail them. Slice into rings about ¼ in. thick. Slice the onion and chop the drained tomatoes roughly. Layer the vegetables, finishing with tomatoes, in a greased 8 in. flameproof casserole, seasoning each layer sparingly with salt and generously with freshly ground black pepper. Sprinkle with breadcrumbs and cover with tiny dabs of the margarine spread. Cover with the lid and bake in a cool oven (160°C, 325°F, Gas 3) for 1½ hours or until the okra is tender. Remove the lid and brown the casserole quickly under the grill.   *Serves 4.*

ORIENTAL SALAD

Crisp bean sprouts, chopped red peppers, tossed with lemon juice and soy sauce

You should be able to buy ready sprouted beans at the greengrocer but, if you have difficulty, buy the dried mung beans from a health-food shop and sprout them yourself. It is easier than growing mustard and cress, because you don't have to grow them on cloth. Put the beans in a jar, cover with cold water, drain and change the water every day. After about 10 days, the beans should have sprouted. This salad is more easily mixed using clean hands rather than forks. Prepare a larger quantity than you need for the meal and store the remainder in the refrigerator for a day or two.

Calories: 30

½ kg (1 lb) bean sprouts　　1 tablespoon fresh lemon
1 red pepper　　　　　　　 juice
salt　　　　　　　　　　　 2 tablespoons soy sauce
pepper

Soak the bean sprouts in cold water for 10 to 15 minutes.
Drain thoroughly and dry on kitchen paper. Core, seed
and chop the red pepper and mix in a large bowl with the
bean sprouts, salt, pepper, lemon juice and soy sauce.
Serves 8.

PLANTERS' SALAD

---

*Shredded lettuce, apple, celery, radishes, green pepper and spring
onions with chopped roasted peanuts, dressed with orange juice
and olive oil*

Roasted peanuts are a terrible slimming hazard, because
they are so moreish. 1 peanut has 5 calories. Include a few
in this salad, for the taste spreads throughout. Use dry
roasted peanuts, not the usual oily kind. You will find this
salad filling and satisfying.

Calories: 60–90 (depending on size of serving)

1 lettuce heart　　　　　　 squeeze fresh lemon
½ dessert apple, cored　　　　 juice
1 celery stalk　　　　　　　 1 tablespoon orange
4 radishes　　　　　　　　 juice
4 spring onions　　　　　　 1 tablespoon olive oil
¼ green pepper　　　　　　 salt
25 g (1 oz) dry roasted　　　 pepper
　peanuts

Shred the lettuce, quarter and slice the apple, slice the
celery thinly and chop the remaining vegetables and nuts.
Combine the juices, oil and seasoning, pour over the salad,
toss thoroughly and turn into a salad bowl. *Serves 4 to 6.*

POACHED CUCUMBER IN WINE SAUCE

Slivers of cucumber cooked with spring onions in a thickened sauce of chicken stock and white wine

Cucumbers – at only 50 calories for the whole vegetable – are obtainable throughout the year, but are cheapest in late summer. Feel the cucumber before you buy and avoid those with soft, bendy ends. Like humans, slim is best. The bulged-out shiny kind have very little flavour. You can liquidize cucumbers for use in soups and store them in the freezer but, because of its high water content, a thawed whole cucumber would not be suitable for salads. As you may have noticed through this section of the book, I have a great respect for vegetables and I believe it is well worth spending the extra calories on a well-dressed vegetable dish for dinner.

Calories: 60

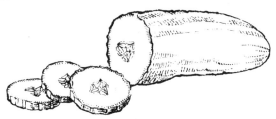

1 large cucumber
4 or 5 slender spring
  onions
15 g (½ oz, 1 tablespoon)
  butter
4 tablespoons chicken
  stock

3 tablespoons dry white
  wine
salt
pepper
1 teaspoon cornflour
1 tablespoon freshly
  chopped parsley (optional)

Top and tail the cucumber, but do not peel. Cut into quarters lengthwise, then slice thinly. (Do not use a food processor which produces paper-thin slices.) Chop the spring onions and sauté in the butter until soft. Add the cucumber, turning carefully with a palette knife until the cucumber is coated. Pour in the stock, wine and a light sprinkle of salt and pepper. Cover with a lid and cook gently until the cucumber is tender – about 5 minutes. Using a slotted spoon, transfer the vegetables to a heated serving dish. Blend the cornflour with 2 tablespoons cold water. Mix with the liquid left in the saucepan and cook, stirring continuously, until the sauce thickens – about 1 minute. Season to taste, then pour sauce over the cucumber and sprinkle with the parsley. *Serves 4.*

POACHED FENNEL

Wedges of fennel root cooked in lemon juice and glazed with butter

Fennel has a slightly minty, aniseedy taste with a hint of celery flavour. Crisp and fresh in salads, but equally refreshing when poached in lemon juice.

Calories: 30

2 large fennel roots	salt
1 tablespoon fresh lemon juice	pepper
	1 teaspoon butter

Wash the fennel roots. Remove a slice from the bottom and cut off the tips and outside leaves. Cut each fennel root into eight wedges and put them in a saucepan with the lemon juice. Barely cover with water, season with salt and pepper and add the butter. Bring to the boil, then lower the heat, cover tightly and poach for about 30 minutes until tender but still slightly crisp. Drain thoroughly and arrange in a heated serving dish. *Serves 4.*

RUSSIAN SLIVERED PEPPERS

Green and red pepper rings in a sugar and vinegar sauce –
served cold

This unusually flavoured dish should be tried out on the
family before you decide if it is suitable for guests. I hasten
to point out that this sweet and sour sauce is not to everybody's taste. You could cut down on the sugar if you wish
or use just 1 teaspoon (to save 50 calories) and add liquid
sweetener while chilling.

Calories : 80

4 medium green peppers	1 tablespoon demerara
4 medium red peppers	sugar
1 tablespoon wine vinegar	1 teaspoon salt
6 bay leaves	1 dozen black peppercorns

Seed and core the peppers and cut into $\frac{1}{2}$ in. rings. Put
them in a saucepan with the vinegar, bay leaves, sugar and
salt. Stir in the peppercorns, slightly bruised with the head
of a rolling pin. Add barely sufficient water to cover the
peppers and simmer until just tender – about 10 minutes.
Transfer the pepper rings to a serving dish. Raise the heat
under the saucepan and boil until the liquid is reduced to
3 or 4 tablespoons. Strain over the peppers and chill for 2
to 3 hours.   *Serves 4.*

SKEWERED VEGETABLES

Chunks of courgettes, whole mushrooms and tomatoes – grilled,
sprinkled with cheese and browned quickly

A pretty way to serve vegetables either on their own, on a
bed of rice, with a green salad, or as an accompaniment or
super garnish to a lamb or beef casserole dish. Use four
short skewers or cocktail sticks if these can be pressed into
the vegetables so that the wood does not burn.

Calories: 95

2 × 1 in. thick courgettes	2 tablespoons vegetable oil
salt	15 g (½ oz) Parmesan
8 button mushrooms	cheese, grated
4 small tomatoes	pepper

Put the courgettes into a pan of boiling salted water and cook for 4 minutes. Drain thoroughly. Remove a sliver from the tops and bottoms, then cut each courgette into thick slices. Cut off the mushroom stalks level with the caps. Thread the courgettes, mushrooms and tomatoes on to the skewers, passing the skewers through the skins of the courgettes, the stubby stalks of the mushrooms and the stalk ends of the tomatoes. Brush with oil and grill under medium heat for 6 to 8 minutes, turning the skewers from time to time. Spread the cheese on a large plate and sprinkle with pepper. Dip the skewers into the cheese, then raise the grill heat to maximum and quickly brown on all sides – about 1 minute. *Serves 4.*

SPINACH AND PEPPER CASSEROLE

A dish of baked vegetables, predominantly spinach, with a sauce of tomato juice and grated Cheddar cheese, then browned in a hot oven

Vegetables are often considered the poor relation of meat or fish. This recipe could be served as a main dish on its own with a little rice. On a compensatory day, fold a heaped tablespoon of the hot mixture into a chapatti or pitta (125 calories) and you have a substantial low-calorie meal for 250.

Calories: 130

2 medium green peppers, cored, seeded and quartered
4 celery sticks, halved
2 medium onions, quartered
$\frac{1}{2}$ kg (1 lb) spinach
25 g (1 oz) sultanas, chopped

$\frac{1}{2}$ teaspoon chilli compound powder
$\frac{1}{2}$ teaspoon paprika
pinch sugar
pinch cinnamon
1 teaspoon salt
4 tablespoons tomato juice
25 g (1 oz) Cheddar cheese grated

Boil the peppers, celery and onions until only just tender. Drain and chop finely. Wash the spinach, remove the tough stalks and briefly drain. Put in a tightly lidded saucepan without any extra water and cook over a thread of heat, shaking the pan from time to time. When the spinach is cooked, drain, shred finely and mix with the other vegetables and the sultanas. Turn into a greased ovenproof dish. Stir the seasonings and spices into the tomato juice, pour it over the vegetables and add a light covering of cheese. Bake in a hot oven (220°C, 425°F, Gas 7) for 10 to 15 minutes until brown on top. *Serves 4.*

SWEET AND SOUR ONIONS

Baby onions baked in vinegar, salt and sugar and caramelized in low fat spread

Small onions are far more attractive than the large if additional vegetables are being served. The acids which make you cry are released from the root. Peel the onions from the stalk end, leaving the piece around the root until the last, then slice away the root under cold running water. I find it convenient to do this on a small chopping board placed in the bottom of the sink.

Calories: 80

3 tablespoons white wine
vinegar
1 teaspoon salt
1 teaspoon sugar
3 drops liquid sweetener

½ kg (1 lb) very small
onions, peeled
50 g (2 oz) low-calorie
margarine spread

Mix the vinegar, salt, sugar and sweetener in an ovenproof dish. Add the onions and bake at 180°C, 350°F, Gas 4, for ½ hour. Add the margarine spread and stir until it has melted and the onions are well coated. Bake for a further ½ hour until the onions are tender and much of the liquid evaporated. *Serves 4.*

TOMATO AND AUBERGINE CASSEROLE

Aubergine slices mixed with tomatoes and flavoured with bay leaves and lemon slices

This recipe was so easy that I could hardly believe it could be so delicious. Vary the herbs if you wish – many people like to use oregano (marjoram), the herb that gives a pizza its characteristic flavour. I prefer the basil and bay leaf combination. Serve hot or cold or reheated.

Calories: 45

2 large aubergines
salt
396 g (14 oz) can tomatoes
2 teaspoons dried basil

2 bay leaves
pepper
3 lemon slices

Peel the aubergines, slice thinly and spread out on a plate. Sprinkle with salt and leave for half an hour. Drain, rinse and pat dry, using kitchen paper. Mix in a non-stick pan with the tomatoes, herbs, seasoning and lemon. Cover with a lid and simmer, stirring occasionally until the aubergine is soft and almost pulpy – about 45 minutes. Remove the lemon slices and bay leaves. *Serves 4.*

TOMATO RING

Jellied tomato juice ring mould

The ingredients for this low-calorie tomato ring will be sufficient for a pint ring mould. If you are not sure of the size of a ring you have, fill a milk bottle with water and pour it into the mould. If the water nearly reaches the edge, the size is right. Double the recipe ingredients if you have a larger ring. After unmoulding fill the hole in the middle with a salad of your choice. If you wet the serving dish before turning out the jelly, you will be able to shake it along if it is not positioned centrally.

Calories: 25

454 ml (16 oz) can tomato juice
15 g ($\frac{1}{2}$ oz) powdered gelatine

1 teaspoon fresh lemon juice or few drops Worcestershire sauce
salt
pepper

Rinse the inside of a ring mould with cold water. Shake out the surplus moisture, but do not wipe dry. Heat without boiling 3 tablespoons tomato juice, sprinkle the gelatine over the surface and stir until dissolved. Leave to cool for several minutes but not so long that the mixture begins to set. Mix in the remaining tomato juice, the lemon juice or Worcestershire sauce and stir thoroughly to blend. Season to taste with salt and pepper, then pour into the ring and leave in a cool place, or refrigerate until set. Dip the base of the ring briefly in hot water and turn out on to a dampened dish. *Serves 4.*

6
Desserts

APPLE DUMPLINGS

Chopped apple mixed with the dumpling batter and poached in orange juice

Sometimes it is nice to have a pudding that you can get your teeth into. And you could, without offence, ask for two dumplings (140 calories) only please. If you prefer you can bake the dumplings in a hot oven (220°C, 425°F, Gas 7) on a non-stick baking tray for 10 minutes, turning them over after 7 minutes. You will not then require the sauce.

Calories: 210 (3 dumplings)

100 g (4 oz) self-raising
   flour
1 teaspoon baking powder
40 g (1½ oz) margarine
225 g (8 oz, 2 medium)
   dessert apples

5 tablespoons orange juice
liquid sweetener
few drops yellow food
   colouring

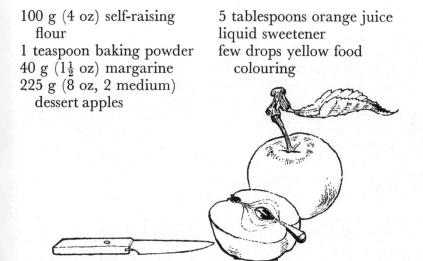

Sieve the flour and baking powder into a bowl and rub in the margarine. Peel, core and chop the apples, add to the mixture and mix in 2 or 3 tablespoons of orange juice to form a soft dough. Half fill a saucepan with water, add sweetener and colouring and bring to the boil. Lower the heat to simmering point. Using a dessert spoon, form the dough into twelve evenly-sized balls and slide into the pan four at a time. Cook until puffy – about 4 minutes – continuously spooning the liquid over the dumplings. Lift the dumplings into a heated serving dish. Cover and keep warm. Add the remaining orange juice to the saucepan and boil rapidly until reduced to a thick sauce. Pour the sauce over the dumplings and serve hot. *Serves 4.*

APPLE SNOW

Sieved apples whipped with egg white and vanilla essence and decorated with toasted almonds

Basic calorie count for this recipe is 95 per serving *but* you can dress it up if you wish. A tablespoon of a liqueur such as Cointreau, Curaçao, Kirsch or apricot brandy mixed into the apple adds only 50 calories between the four glasses. 15 g ($\frac{1}{2}$ oz) plain chocolate, grated, could be sprinkled over the whites for an extra 20 calories each and two tablespoons of beaten whipping cream, coloured green or beige with food colouring, would only add 140 calories and this is enough to provide a nice big rosette on each glass.

Calories: 100

$\frac{1}{2}$ kg (1 lb) dessert apples
1 teaspoon finely grated
   lemon zest
few drops liquid sweetener
2 egg whites

$\frac{1}{2}$ teaspoon vanilla essence
25 g (1 oz) sugar
15 g ($\frac{1}{2}$ oz) flaked almonds,
   toasted

Peel, core and slice the apples and put into a heavy-based saucepan with the lemon zest. Cover tightly and cook over the lowest possible heat until soft. Rub the apples through a sieve and add the liquid sweetener to taste. Leave to cool. Beat the egg whites until soft peaks form and fold just under half the amount into the apples. Continue beating the remainder until really stiff. Add the vanilla essence and sugar and beat until the egg whites are stiff once more. Divide the apples between four sundae glasses and top them with the beaten whites and a sprinkling of almonds.

BLACKCURRANT SOUFFLÉ

Hot baked soufflé dessert

Fresh blackcurrants should be washed and all the woody sprigs removed. Frozen blackcurrants are ready for cooking, but tend to produce more juice so you may not need to add water when stewing. If you wish, you may double the quantities when mixing, but cook in two separate dishes.

Calories: 125

225 g (8 oz) blackcurrants (fresh or frozen)	100 g (4 oz) caster sugar
few drops liquid sweetener	4 or 5 egg whites

Prepare a moderate oven (180°C, 350°F, Gas 4). Lightly grease a 1 l (2 pint) soufflé dish. Put the blackcurrants in a saucepan with not more than 2 tablespoons of water and cook over gentle heat until the fruit is soft but not mushy and about 2 tablespoons of free liquid remains. Add the sweetener and half the sugar. Beat the egg whites until stiff, then add the remainder of the sugar and beat again. Fold the mixture into the fruit and pour into the prepared dish. Bake in the centre of the oven for 30 to 40 minutes until well risen, resisting the temptation to open the oven for the first 20 minutes. Serve at once. *Serves 4.*

BLACKCURRANT WATER ICE

Blackcurrants and lemon juice combined with egg whites and sugar and then frozen

Fresh or frozen blackcurrants are suitable for this recipe, but not the canned variety. So, provided the blackcurrant drink manufacturers have not purchased the entire crop, this recipe can be made at any time. There is plenty of Vitamin C here, so you are not eating just empty calories.

Calories: **140**

275 g (10 oz) blackcurrants
1 teaspoon fresh lemon
 juice

100 g (4 oz) granulated
 sugar
2 large egg whites

Put the blackcurrants in a heavy-based pan with the lemon juice. Cover tightly and cook over the lowest possible heat until the fruit is soft. Give the pan a shake from time to time to prevent sticking. Press through a sieve and make up the purée to 600 ml (1 pint) with water. Dissolve the sugar in 300 ml ($\frac{1}{2}$ pint)water and, without covering, bring to the boil and cook rapidly for 5 to 10 minutes until a thick syrup is formed. Mix with the purée. Leave to cool, then put in a shallow dish in the freezer. Leave until half frozen – 1 to 2 hours. Whip the egg whites until stiff and fold into the iced purée. Open freeze and, if not required within a few hours, cover tightly. Remove from the freezer 20 to 30 minutes before serving, then transfer to a chilled dish with an ice-cream scoop. *Serves 4.*

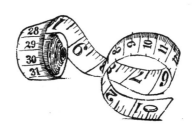

BLACKBERRY AND STRAWBERRY JELLIES

Layers of fruit and jelly served in sundae glasses and topped with cream rosettes

Not for one minute would I suggest that frozen fruit is superior to fresh fruit – but in this recipe I have chosen frozen for two reasons. Firstly it produces the fruit juice which is necessary for the jelly, and secondly by using frozen I can marry two seasonal fruits that are rarely in the shops fresh at the same time.

Calories: 30

225 g (8 oz) frozen
  blackberries
225 g (8 oz) frozen
  strawberries
150 to 200 ml (5 to 7 fl. oz)
  fresh orange juice

2 level teaspoons powdered
  gelatine
few drops liquid sweetener
4 rosettes whipped cream
  (pre-frozen, see page
  143)

Leave the fruit in separate covered bowls at room temperature until completely thawed. Strain the juice into a wide-necked measuring jug. Set the fruits aside. Make up to just under 250 ml (½ pint) with orange juice. Sprinkle the gelatine into two tablespoons of hot water, stirring until dissolved. Leave to cool, then pour into the fruit juice, stirring vigorously. Add liquid sweetener to taste and refrigerate until the jelly is just on the point of setting. Divide the strawberries between four sundae glasses. Cover with a layer of jelly and put back in the refrigerator. As soon as the jelly sets, top up with the blackberries and a single rosette of cream. *Serves 4.*

CHEESE AND APPLE SOUFFLÉ

Curd cheese and cooking apples lightened with egg yolk and beaten whites and baked in a moderate oven

Would you believe that you could eat soufflé on a slimming budget? This recipe only has one egg yolk but will be even better if you can spare the calories for one more. I have used Granny Smith's, but you could substitute cooking apples which are cheaper but would need a little more sweetener.

Calories: 75

½ kg (1 lb) green dessert apples
100 g (**3 oz**) curd cheese
1 large egg, plus 2 whites

few drops liquid sweetener
1 teaspoon flour

Peel and core the apples. Dice finely, put into a tightly lidded non-stick saucepan and stew over the lowest possible heat until soft. Purée in the liquidizer or press through a sieve. Beat in the cheese, egg yolk, sweetener and flour. Whisk the 3 egg whites in a grease-free bowl until stiff. Stir one spoonful into the apple mixture, then fold in the remainder. Generously fill 6 individual greased 7 in. ramekin dishes with the mixture and bake in the centre of a pre-heated moderate oven (180°C, 350°F, Gas 4) for 10 to 12 minutes until risen and golden brown. Serve immediately. *Serves 6.*

CHEESE AND RAISIN PANCAKES

Pancakes filled with soaked raisins, curd cheese and spice and heated in fresh orange juice

To make low-calorie pancakes you must have a non-stick pan. Make use of an existing frying pan but, if you have to buy a new one, select a 7 in. omelette pan. The curved edges make it easier to slide a palette knife under the pancakes. One pancake only please for the slimmer.

Calories: 150 each pancake

Pancakes

100 g (4 oz) plain flour
pinch salt
1 large egg

300 ml ($\frac{1}{2}$ pint) skimmed milk
1 teaspoon vegetable oil

Filling

juice and grated rind of 1 large orange
40 g (1$\frac{1}{2}$ oz) raisins
200 g (7 oz) curd cheese

25 g (1 oz) icing sugar
pinch ground mixed spice
few drops liquid sweetener (optional)

Make up the pancake batter in the usual way, by beating together all the ingredients except the oil. Set aside. To prepare the filling, combine the orange juice, rind and raisins. Leave to soak for approximately 2 hours – this is particularly necessary if you have had the raisins in the larder for some time. When they are nicely plumped up, remove them from the juice with a slotted spoon and mix with the cheese, sugar and spice. Taste, adding a few drops of liquid sweetener if desired. Now make eight pancakes, brushing the pan only once with oil before starting. Divide the filling into eight and pile one portion on to one half of each pancake. This will prevent the mixture from oozing out when the pancake is rolled up. Roll up each pancake and arrange on a flameproof dish. Pour the orange juice and rind over them, cover with foil and warm under the grill well away from the element or flame. *Serves 4.*

CHILLED COFFEE SOUFFLÉ

A cold mousse-like coffee dessert

Go easy on the decoration as chocolate vermicelli have 135 calories per ounce. Chopped hazelnuts have 180 calories and two grated chocolate wholemeal biscuits contain 150 calories. Chill the can of milk for 1 or 2 hours before whipping. Since these are modestly sized portions, they look better served in individual dishes.

Calories: 160 (without decoration)

2 eggs, separated
2 tablespoons sugar
150 ml ($\frac{1}{4}$ pint) double-strength black coffee, warm
1 tablespoon powdered gelatine

171 g (6 oz) can evaporated milk
vanilla essence
25 g (1 oz) grated chocolate, nuts or biscuits
4 individual soufflé dishes

Securely fit greaseproof paper collars protruding one inch above each soufflé dish. Beat the egg yolks and sugar to a thick cream, then add half the coffee, beating vigorously until thick. Sprinkle the gelatine on to the remaining coffee, stirring until dissolved. Stir this into the creamed mixture and put aside until on the point of setting. Flavour the undiluted milk with vanilla essence and beat until thick. Wash the beaters to remove all traces of grease, then whisk the egg whites to stiff peaks. Stir the milk into the coffee jelly and fold the whites in with a large metal spoon. Pour into the dishes and refrigerate until set. To remove the collars slide a hot bladed knife between the paper and the dish. Decorate sparingly for the slimmer.   *Serves 4.*

CREAM ROSETTES

Decorations for sweet or savoury dishes

Double cream (130 calories per fluid ounce) or whipping cream (105 calories per fluid ounce) are both suitable for whipping. I find that double cream keeps its shape better when frozen as rosettes and makes little difference in the calorie value of a single rosette. Cream must be whipped carefully, particularly if you use an electric beater. One moment it appears too soft and the next you find it has curdled and you now have not cream but butter and a milky fluid. While neither need be wasted, it was cream that you required, so you won't be too pleased. You may find it easier to use a hand-operated rotary whisk. Beat the cream until it is really thick, particularly if the decorations have to stand at room temperature for some time. Put the whipped cream into a forcing bag or piping device fitted with a ½ in. star nozzle. Pipe rosettes as required.

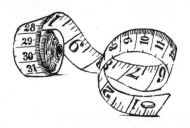

To freeze: Pipe rosettes of cream on to a tray lined with greaseproof paper and open freeze. When the rosettes are completely frozen, leaving them in place, cut the paper into pieces to fit your freezer box. Layer carefully and seal the box. Store for up to two months and when required the rosettes may be transferred with a palette knife to the dishes requiring decoration. The rosettes will take very little time to thaw since they are so small.

FRESH FRUIT SALAD

A mixture of fresh fruits sweetened with fruit juice

Always serve a fresh fruit salad as an alternative dessert. It is remarkable how many of your guests will plump for it. Allow one whole fruit per person. The larger the number of guests, therefore, the greater the variety of fruit that can be introduced. Dry fruit salad does not keep very well but, if bathed in sugar syrup, which the slimmer must avoid, or well moistened with a citrus fruit juice, it can be used up day after day for as long as a week, provided it is kept in the refrigerator, uncovered and tossed each day.

Calories: 50

A choice of 8 items from the list below:

1 orange	50 g (2 oz) blackberries
100 g (4 oz) green dessert apple	100 g (4 oz) cherries
	4 apricots
100 g (4 oz) red dessert apple	50 g (2 oz) slice of pineapple
100 g (4 oz) pear	8 tablespoons unsweetened
175 g (6 oz) banana	orange or grapefruit juice
8 grapes -	liquid sweetener (optional)

To prepare, oranges should be segmented without the pith, apples cored and cut into chunks but not peeled. The skin on pears is rather tough, so peel, core, then cut up. Bananas are best cut in quarters lengthwise then sliced into thick pieces. Leave the skins on grapes, but remove the pips with a clean, sterilized crochet hook or hair-grip. Stone cherries and apricots and cut the pineapple slice into small wedges. Pour the fruit juice, laced with a few drops of liquid sweetener if liked, over the fruit and toss to prevent it darkening. Chill until required. *Serves 8.*

FRESH PEACH AND RASPBERRY DESSERT

Peaches poached in grapefruit juice and bedded in fresh raspberry jelly

Please use fresh peaches, but frozen raspberries, first thawed, can replace the fresh variety. If the peaches are small, you could use six instead of the four shown in the recipe. This dessert keeps well for several days so, if you are doing much entertaining, you could double up the ingredients and prepare two separate dishes.

Calories: 80

4 ripe peaches
150 ml (¼ pint)
  unsweetened grapefruit
  juice
1 teaspoon powdered
  gelatine

liquid sweetener
350 g (12 oz) raspberries
1 egg white
1 teaspoon sugar

Plunge the peaches into boiling water, switch off the heat and leave for two minutes. Remove one at a time, briefly run them under cold water, then press away the skin with the thumbs. Put the peaches in a dry saucepan with the grapefruit juice. Cover tightly with a lid and poach gently for 15 to 20 minutes until just tender. Hasten the process by turning the fruit over once during the cooking time. Using a slotted spoon, transfer the peaches to a serving dish. Switch off the heat under the pan, sprinkle on the gelatine, stirring briskly until dissolved. Sweeten to taste, then stir in the raspberries. Crush lightly. Leave to cool. Whip the egg white until stiff, then add the sugar to stabilize and whisk again. Fold carefully into the raspberries and spoon around the peaches. Refrigerate until required.
Serves 4.

JAPANESE CHEESECAKE

Authentic oriental cheese cake without crust on the bottom

We call it cheesecake, but it doesn't look like the traditional continental kind. I used green label Speiselquark – 88 calories per 100 g (3½ oz) – but you can substitute any low-calorie soft cheese.

Calories: 170

1 packet lemon jelly
1 medium lemon
225 g (8 oz) Speiselquark
  cheese

25 g (1 oz) sultanas
4 sweetmeal (digestive)
  biscuits, crushed

Melt the jelly in 150 ml (¼ pint) almost boiling water. Grate the lemon rind, then cut in half and squeeze the juice. Add the grated lemon rind and lemon juice to the dissolved jelly, then whisk in the cheese. Pour mixture into a 6 in. shallow tin and refrigerate. When nearly set, sprinkle with the sultanas and crushed biscuits. *Serves 4.*

LEMON FLUFF

Whipped-up lemon jelly with fresh cream decoration

Recipes need not be complicated to produce attractive and exciting dishes. This tried and tested jelly dessert will receive acclaim if the simple instructions are followed carefully. The slimmer can skilfully serve herself a cream-free portion.

Calories: 130–160 (depending on size of serving) – excludes the cream topping

171 g (6 oz) can evaporated
  milk
1 lemon jelly

1 large juicy lemon
150 ml (¼ pint) cream

Refrigerate the can of evaporated milk for several hours or put it in the freezer for half an hour. Place the jelly in 300 ml (½ pint) hot, but not boiling, water and stir until dissolved. Leave until cool, but not set. Meanwhile, slice the lemon very very thinly, discard the ends and put the remainder in a non-stick pan with 2 tablespoons water and cook over a thread of heat until the peel just breaks with light pressure from the back of a knife. Turn the lemon slices over once during cooking. Choose a serving dish that complements the lemon colour and arrange half the lemon slices in the base. Whisk the chilled milk until frothy then, while continuing to whisk, pour in the jelly from a height. The mixture will now be creamy and frothy. Pour it over the lemon slices in the dish and leave until set, when all the little bubbles on top will have popped. Whip the cream until thick, transfer it to a piping bag fitted with a ½ in. star nozzle and pipe rosettes of cream on to the set jelly. Decorate with the remaining lemon slices cut into wedges. *Serves 4 to 5.*

MERINGUES WITH FRENCH CUSTARD FILLING

Tiny meringues sandwiched with well-flavoured pastry cream

Yes – meringues! You have to use sugar, but it is cheaper on calories than cakes using butter. Before starting make sure that you are working in a dry atmosphere. Follow the rules for beating and you will get greater volume and produce larger meringues. The very best method is to use a copper-lined bowl and an enormous balloon whisk. Beating by hand with a loop whisk in a non-shiny bowl is the next best. Add a pinch of cream of tartar and make sure you lift the whisk high above the mixture with every revolution. When the whites are thick but not yet dry, add less than half the sugar and this time whisk until really stiff. You have reached the right stiffness when peaks picked up with the whisk keep their shape. Lastly sprinkle in the remaining sugar so that it lands over the whole of the surface area and *fold* in with a metal tablespoon, sweeping the spoon under the mixture, bringing it up one side and cutting through the middle on the down stroke. Meringues grow during baking, so start off with them as small as you like.

For filling you could use low-calorie ice cream (30 calories per portion) or ordinary ice cream (55 calories per portion). Sandwich with crushed raspberries and yogurt (25 calories) and fill some with a fattening dollop of whipped cream for non-dieters. Don't put the filling in until the last moment or the meringues will soften. You may also care to try the filling below.

Calories: 100 per 2 large meringue halves plus 40 for the filling

2 large egg whites at room   pinch cream of tartar
   temperature   100 g (4 oz) caster sugar

Filling   ¼ teaspoon vanilla essence
150 ml (¼ pint) skimmed   1 large egg yolk
   milk   liquid sweetener
1 tablespoon flour

To make the meringues beat the egg whites and cream of tartar in a grease-free bowl with a spotlessly clean whisk. When the whites are fairly stiff, add less than half the sugar and beat until the mixture is stiff and shiny. Fold in the remaining sugar. Arrange 8 tablespoons of meringue well spaced out on a lightly greased non-stick baking tray or on a tray lined with non-stick paper. Bake in a slow oven

(150°C, 300°F, Gas 2) for 1 to 2 hours until the meringues are crisp on top and can be lifted easily from the tray when loosened with a fish slice. While the meringues are baking, make the filling. Put the milk in a saucepan, add the flour, vanilla essence and egg yolk and mix thoroughly. Cook over very low heat, whisking continuously until the sauce thickens. Sweeten to taste. Transfer to a bowl, cover with a piece of cling film and chill until the sauce is the consistency of thick custard. Fill meringues when cool. *Serves 4.*

PANCAKE CIGARS

Four-inch pancakes filled with chocolate mousse and topped with cream

The portions are small but delicious and make a change from the monotonous low-calorie desserts you force on yourself.

Calories: 65 (per cigar)

Batter

100 g (4 oz) plain flour
pinch salt
1 large egg
300 ml ($\frac{1}{2}$ pint) skimmed
  milk

2 drops liquid sweetener
1 teaspoon orange flower
  water

Other Ingredients

1 teaspoon vegetable oil
85 g (3 oz) Sainsbury's
  chocolate mousse

4 tablespoons single
  cream

Prepare the pancake batter, thinning it down if necessary with water. Brush a small non-stick pan with oil and make fourteen or fifteen 4 in. pancakes, oiling the pan once after every five pancakes. Keep the pancakes warm until all are cooked. Place a sliver of mousse on the edge of each pancake and roll up like cigars. Arrange in a warm serving dish and pour the cream over. Serve four to each non-slimmer. *Serves 4.*

RUBY PEARS

Pear halves poached in orange juice and red wine – served in a thickened sauce and decorated with toasted almonds

This is one of those adaptable recipes which enable you to double up, halve or change at will. Add ground allspice or cloves to the liquid, use apples and bottled apple juice and perk it up with a tablespoon of Grand Marnier. But, however you alter the ingredients, do not alter the proportion of arrowroot to liquid, as this would spoil the correct consistency for the sauce. Serve with sponge finger biscuits which have 20 calories each.

Calories: 115

·2 large, sweet oranges
4 firm dessert pears
150 ml (¼ pint) sweet red
  wine
2 teaspoons – 7 g (¼ oz)
  arrowroot

few drops liquid sweetener
25 g (1 oz) flaked almonds,
  well toasted

Wash and dry the oranges. Pare the thinnest outside layer of the rind and cut into strips. Halve the oranges and squeeze out the juice. Peel, halve and core the pears and put into a saucepan with the orange juice, the strips of rind and the wine. Cook until the pears are just tender – 10–15 minutes. Remove the pears to a serving dish using a slotted spoon. Measure the liquid left in the saucepan and make up to 250 ml (½ pint) with water. Add the arrowroot, first blended with 2 tablespoons cold water. Bring to the boil, stirring all the time until the sauce clears. Sweeten and pour over the pears. Sprinkle with the toasted almonds.
Serves 4.

STUFFED ORANGES

Orange shells filled with a mixture of stewed apple, raisins and cream flavoured with cardamom and topped with grated chocolate

It doesn't matter which oranges you use provided they are juicy and as sweet as possible. Buy as soon as they appear in the shops. Shipments are infrequent, so it makes sense when we are told that the longer they are stored, the dryer they become. In other words it is better to buy a young Jaffa than an old Spanish or vice versa. If you can spare the calories, pipe a rosette of beaten whipping cream on to each orange (about 40 more calories per serving).

Calories: 165

2 juicy oranges
½ kg (1 lb, 2 large) cooking
  apples
2 tablespoons sugar
2 tablespoons seedless
  raisins
1 teaspoon ground
  cardamom
¼ teaspoon almond essence
liquid sweetener
1 tablespoon double
  cream

6 squares milk chocolate
  grated

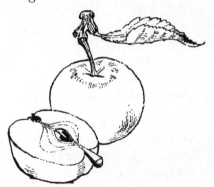

Squeeze the juice from the oranges. Reserve the shells. Peel, core and chop the apples and put in a saucepan with the orange juice, sugar, raisins, cardamom and almond essence. Cook gently until the apples are mushy and the juice absorbed. Add liquid sweetener if the mixture is too sharp. Leave to cool, stir in the cream and divide the mixture between the four orange shells. Sprinkle with the chocolate. *Serves 4.*

TIPSY BERRIES

Fresh raspberries and redcurrants soaked for several hours in wine and brandy

Preferably use a shallow dish for this recipe as this will help the alcohol penetrate the fruit.

Calories: 120

1 tablespoon sugar
300 ml ($\frac{1}{2}$ pint, 2 glasses)
   sweet red wine
4 tablespoons brandy

$\frac{1}{2}$ kg (1 lb) raspberries –
   fresh or frozen
225 g (8 oz) redcurrants
liquid sweetener

Mix the sugar with the wine and brandy. Pick over the fruit and remove all the bits of branch from the redcurrants. Put fruit into a dish, pour the syrup over it and chill for several hours, stirring carefully from time to time. Add sweetener if required.   *Serves 4.*

VANILLA SPONGE CAKE

Fatless low-calorie sponge cake

Use an electric mixer to produce this 80-calorie-a-slice vanilla sponge cake. Preparation time is no more than 5 minutes and the cake is baked in 12. You can use a 1 lb loaf tin, but I have a collection of foil containers salvaged from take-away curries. The folding-in process is important for a light cake and this is also the reason for pouring and *not* spooning the mixture into the baking tin.

Calories: 80

2 large (size 1 or 2) eggs
pinch cream of tartar
25 g (1 oz) caster sugar

$\frac{1}{2}$ teaspoon vanilla essence
50 g (2 oz) plain flour

Prepare a fairly hot oven (200°C, 400°F, Gas 6). Beat the eggs and cream of tartar and sugar until thick and mousse-like – when a fork drawn through the mixture leaves a channel. Stir in the vanilla essence. Sieve the flour from a height over the entire surface of the mixture and fold in briskly. Pour into a lightly greased 1 lb loaf tin, gently tipping the tin to spread the mixture evenly. Bake on the centre shelf for 12 to 15 minutes until resilient to the touch. Do not open the oven for the first 10 minutes. *Serves 6 generously.*

THICK HOME-MADE YOGURT

The Indians call it *'dahi'*, the Greeks know it as *'yaorti'*, in Bulgaria it is *'kisselo mleko'*, but to the Englishman it is 'yogurt'. When yogurt first appeared in the shops it was natural flavour only. In the early sixties yogurt appeared in sweetened fruit-flavoured form. Lately it has become more expensive and no doubt further price rises will result from the rising cost of milk. You can make it yourself using a tablespoon of commercial natural yogurt and a pint of milk. But for absolute success you must obey two vital rules:

1 All utensils must be absolutely germ-free – a rinse with a Milton solution will ensure this.

2 The temperature of the milk must be between 32° and 46°C (90° and 115°F) when the culture is added. Use a cooking thermometer to be sure, or test by dropping a few drops on to the inside of your wrist. This should feel warm, but not hot. This temperature will then be maintained in a yogurt-maker or a vacuum flask. After eight hours, test for setting. The mixture should be lightly set. Empty into small plastic pots, cover and put in the refrigerator to finish setting.

Home made yogurt will only keep for 2 or 3 days. The following recipe makes just under 1 pint and has 380 calories.

450 ml (¾ pint) full cream U H T (long-life) milk
1 heaped tablespoon dried skimmed milk
1 generous tablespoon natural, low-fat yogurt

Put the liquid milk into a large saucepan, bring to the boil, then lower the heat and simmer for 5 minutes. When the milk boils, the protein hardens and forms a lid, preventing the escape of steam and hence it boils over. So push the skin away from the edge from time to time while simmering. Switch off the heat, stir in the milk powder and leave to cool until the milk feels comfortable to the touch. Whisk in the yogurt and immediately pour into a 1 pint flask. Seal, and check the time. After 8 hours open the flask and, if it is ready, pour it into pots and refrigerate for at least 2 hours.

You can make yogurt from skimmed milk only, when the calorific value would be only 200 calories per pint. The result would be much thinner. Bring the milk to the boil, then switch off the heat, leave until just warm to the touch, whisk in a tablespoon of low-fat, natural yogurt and continue as before.

FRUIT YOGURT

Stir chopped fruit into your home-made yogurt, then sweeten to taste before potting.

7
Planning the Menus

Guests for the weekend will not upset the hostess' low-calorie breakfast, but she will have to take more care at lunch, dinner and, perish the thought, teatime. My weekend guests have to help themselves to breakfast and the night before I make sure that everything is ready to hand. Offer a plate of biscuits and coffee mid-morning, including a few Rich Tea, Osborne or Marie amongst the chocolate digestives. Saturday lunch may be a quick, salad-type meal, followed by cheese and fresh fruit. Teatime is difficult and you will have to exercise tremendous won't-power while guests consume crumpets and buttered scones. To be sociable you will have to have at least one of these (75 calories each without adornment) and spread it sparingly with low-calorific margarine. To compensate, cut out the milk in your tea and save 20 calories.

Dinner should present no problem, as you will be able to select menus from this book which should not involve you in eating more than 1000 calories. On Sunday you will probably be cooking our traditional roast and two veg followed by some sort of pastry dish. You should add another vegetable and a salad to the repertoire and prepare an additional low-calorie fruity dessert. If you serve a midday dinner and your guests are still with you in the evening, an open-sandwich meal will do nicely. Remember, one slice is better than two and yours can be unbuttered. Include a few crispbreads, topped at the last moment so they don't go soft. Offer coffee with cream separately.

Informal suppers should give the impression that they were easy to prepare, even if this is not strictly the case. You need not serve three courses, although this is always possible if you are in the habit of keeping plenty of fresh fruit in the house. If fruit is to be the dessert, then you should not serve a fruit starter but a simple well-dressed salad – tomato or cucumber salad is always acceptable. Keep cans of low-calorie soups in the larder – consommé is my favourite – and add other ingredients to them, for example diced vegetables, noodles or a spoonful of cream.

Nearly all the main courses and vegetables in this book are easy to prepare and, if you wish, you can double up on one of the lunch/supper dishes. The advantage of the informal main course is that you can serve plain, home-cooked food without added fat: grilled chops, steaks, poached or grilled fish, or even a vegetarian meal, provided you don't use too much cheese. If you have started with a salad, then you must serve plain vegetables as an accompaniment to the main course. Otherwise salads are very suitable for this purpose and these can be the dressy part of the meal.

Salads and fruit (except bananas) keep well in the bottom of the refrigerator – sometimes called the crisper. This is the least cold area in the refrigerator. When arranged in a basket or glamorous dish with the apples and oranges well shined, nothing could be more appetizing than fruit as a dessert. You can work out the calorie content for this type of uncomplicated meal very easily from the charts in the last section of the book.

At a dinner party you, as hostess, are only calorifically concerned with one meal. You will find a selection of tasty and attractive dishes in the relevant sections. When choosing your menu you may wish to change the garnishes to avoid too much repetition. Make the table as decorative as you can and check that the lighting is 'soft'. It is much less embarrassing to serve yourself a small portion when there is no bright centre light to reveal all.

DINNER MENU SUGGESTIONS

Dishes marked with an asterisk are not in the book as they are everyday recipes.

Menu One

Melon Eliott

–

Limburg Veal
Mashed Potato*
Creamed Chicory
Lettuce and Walnut Salad

–

Blackberry and Strawberry Jellies

Slimmer's Portion: 840 calories

Menu Two

Chicken and Egg Drop Soup

–

Cold Roast Beef*
Tomato Ring filled with Green Salad
Planter's Salad
Broccoli Salad
Carrot Mint Salad

–

Cheese and Raisin Pancakes

Slimmer's Portion: 685 calories

Menu Three

Honolulu Cocktail

–

Salt-Baked Chicken
Poached Fennel
Boiled New Potatoes*
Marrow Lombardia

–

Tipsy Berries

Slimmer's Portion: 635 calories

Menu Four

Tomato Cocottes

—

Sole Rossoverde
Duchesse Potatoes
Green Beans*
Green Salad*

—

Blackcurrant Water Ice

Slimmer's Portion: 645 calories

Menu Five

Pink Prawn Dip

—

Steak de Provence
Oriental Salad
Jacket Potato

—

Fresh Fruit Salad

Slimmer's portion: 520 calories

Menu Six

American Grapefruit

—

Red-Cooked Beef with Cucumber Sheaves
Boiled Rice garnished with Peeled Shrimps*

—

Japanese Cheesecake

Slimmer's portion: 760 calories

Menu Seven

Chicken-Stuffed Mushrooms

–

Lemon Kebabs
Boiled Rice*
Spinach and Pepper Casserole

–

Pancake Cigars

Slimmer's portion: 725 calories

Menu Eight

Tomato and Bacon Soup

–

Pork Medley
Bulgarian Sweetcorn
Poached Cucumber in Wine Sauce

–

Cheese and Apple Soufflé

Slimmer's portion: 465 calories

Menu Nine

Danish Cucumber

–

Tournedos Montpensier
Chopped Spinach*
Duchesse Potatoes

–

Stuffed Oranges

Slimmer's portion: 635 calories

Menu Ten

Avocado Prawn and Grapefruit Cocktail

–

Spit-Roast Pork with Apple Sauce
Red Cabbage*
Braised Celery*
Roast Potatoes (not for the slimmer)

–

Chilled Coffee Soufflé

Slimmer's portion: 575 calories

Menu Eleven

Melon with Parma Ham

–

Crab and Cucumber Layered Crêpes
Courgettes and Lettuce Sauté
Grilled Tomatoes*

–

Meringues with French Custard Filling

Slimmer's portion: 490 calories

Menu Twelve

Peach Overture

–

Norwegian Cured Salmon
Green Salad*
Tomato Salad*
Russian Slivered Peppers
Potato Salad (not for the slimmer)*

–

Lemon Fluff
Vanilla Sponge Cake

Slimmer's portion: 570 calories

PART TWO

How to Compensate

If you come away from your night out feeling you've over-done it, don't worry. You are not the only one who ever over-indulged. You can easily remedy this by compensating with one low-calorie meal and a few snackettes. The recipes are for one or two people, but can be increased easily.

On the day before or after your dinner date, you will have to reduce your calorie intake to balance the books. It is preferable to do this before, because then you have the meal to look forward to. An unexpected invitation could create problems and, if the notice is short, you could, if necessary, exist for a day on lemon tea, coffee and three apples. After all going without food for eight hours occasionally never hurt anyone. If you are inclined to headaches after fasting, you should obviously not starve before your evening out.

Unless you are on a very strict régime, you could have 400 calories before going out without spoiling your diet. None of the recipes in this section is over 400 calories, enabling you to choose which meals you prefer and when to eat them. There is a low-calorie snackette list on page 200. On the day following your binge allow yourself 750 calories, since to drop below that level is unsatisfactory and does not achieve any greater weight loss. After that compensatory day you must return to your normal day's calorie intake, otherwise you are likely to suffer ill-health or become so fed up that you abandon your slimming attempts.

The meals can be taken at the times you feel the most need, and calorie intake can be distributed throughout the day. It depends on which is your most ravenous time. A good breakfast may take you through until dinnertime provided you have a low-calorie drink midday and mid-afternoon. If you are a no-breakfast person, it may suit you better to have a 'substantial lunch' and a light evening meal. I have received conflicting advice from experienced slimmers and some tell me that, if you make up your mind to prepare a perfect, though low-calorie, meal, it will take so long that you won't have time to think about being hungry. This is surely rubbish, for how can anybody be in the kitchen for more than a few minutes without nibbling? My view is that preparation should be fairly speedy, though it is important to cook a reasonable meal. Do all the available washing-up before eating. Put the exact quantity including butter, milk for coffee etc. on a tray, take it out of the kitchen, firmly close the door *and don't go back* until it's time to prepare the next meal.

I
Breakfasts

Many nutritionists believe that it is important to start the day with some sort of meal, since 10 to 12 hours have passed since the last one. The fast caused by lack of calorie intake leaves energy levels low and, as soon as food is absorbed into the system, these levels will rise, giving a feeling of well-being. Breakfast should consist of a quarter of the day's calories and be sufficiently satisfying to catch up on the overnight fast and stave off fatigue. Carbohydrates provide instant energy; proteins and fats take longer to digest and so maintain a fuller feeling. So slimmers are advised to eat breakfast to avoid overcompensatory eating at lunchtime.

An ideal breakfast contains milk, fruit, bread and butter or margarine. But, if you have never been accustomed to breakfasting, your stomach won't appreciate the sudden invasion first thing in the morning. Having said that, even no-breakfast people should have a cup of tea or coffee with milk to give sufficient nutriment to help overcome inertia. If before you started dieting you were not a breakfast eater, there is little point in changing routines and waking up your tummy when it is happily sleeping. You may have been used to a snack in the middle of the morning and your 'appestat' will still expect a refill at this time, whether it has had a newly enforced breakfast or not. Until it settles down your stomach will have to be placated with bulky but low-calorie food. Office workers should take a packed snack to prevent the temptation to accept biscuits offered with the morning coffee.

If you propose to eat a hearty breakfast, work out whether the day is to be a low-calorie compensatory one or a full 1000 to 1500 calorie allowance diet. On the following chart are all the usual breakfast dishes, including one or two all-in-one drinks. Try to choose those with more fat and protein than carbohydrates. The fruit and juices provide enough Vitamin C for a day's requirements. Remember you can have Frosties or Sugar Puffs for the same calorific value as cornflakes, and then you won't be tempted to have any sugar. Use liquid sweetener whenever you wish. Remember that all spoonsful are level.

	Calories to the nearest 5
120 ml (4 fl. oz) glass unsweetened grapefruit juice	40
120 ml (4 fl. oz) glass unsweetened orange juice	40
120 ml (4 fl. oz) natural pineapple juice	65
120 ml (4 fl. oz) tomato juice	30
120 ml (4 fl. oz) apple juice	50
120 ml (4 fl. oz) slightly sweetened lemon juice	20
½ fresh grapefruit	15
cup of tea with 2 tablespoons whole milk	20
cup of coffee with 1 level teaspoon coffee creamer	10
cup of tea with 2 tablespoons skimmed milk	10
150 ml (5 fl. oz) glass whole milk	100
150 ml (5 fl. oz) glass skimmed milk	50
2 tablespoons cornflakes	100
25 g (1 oz) cornflakes with 5 tablespoons skimmed milk	130
25 g (1 oz) cornflakes with 5 tablespoons whole milk	155
3 tablespoons All Bran with 5 tablespoons skimmed milk	85
3 tablespoons All Bran with 5 tablespoons whole milk	110
1 Shredded Wheat	70
1 Weetabix	50
25 g (1 oz) muesli with 5 tablespoons apple juice	130
6 tablespoons porridge made with whole milk	160
6 tablespoons porridge made with skimmed milk	110

6 tablespoons porridge made with water	80
poached egg size 5 cooked in water	70
soft-boiled egg size 5	70
scrambled eggs, 2, size 6, scrambled with 2 tablespoons skimmed milk	150
1 grilled back-bacon rasher	65
1 well-pricked grilled sausage	105
1 well-pricked grilled chipolata sausage	80
50 g (2 oz) boiled ham and 1 tomato	130
1 medium tomato, grilled without butter	10
1 small kipper 100 ml (4 oz)	120
100 ml (1–4 oz) portion smoked-haddock fillet, steamed without butter	120
2 Ryvitas spread with 7 g ($\frac{1}{4}$ oz) Outline	75
2 Energen crispbread spread with 15 g ($\frac{1}{2}$ oz) Dairylea cheese spread	75
1 thin slice toast spread with 7 g ($\frac{1}{4}$ oz) Outline	95
1 thin slice dry white bread	70
1 teaspoon marmalade or jam	25
$\frac{1}{2}$ teaspoon Marmite or yeast extract	5

BLACKCURRANT BREAKFAST

Use fresh or frozen fruit and fresh or canned orange juice. If you use frozen fruit and dislike very cold drinks, this can be made the night before or heated gently. The wheatgerm is included for added vitamins.

Calories: 120 (per serving)

75 g (3 oz) blackcurrants, trimmed
150 ml ($\frac{1}{4}$ pint) orange juice
1 teaspoon wheatgerm

1 teaspoon sunflower oil
2 rounded teaspoons clear honey
1 size 6 egg

Put all the ingredients into the liquidizer goblet and switch on at medium speed for $1\frac{1}{2}$ minutes. Serve at once. *Serves 2.*

FRESH FRUIT JUICE

The juice of one large (50 calories) or two small (60 calories) oranges serves one person.

The juice of one grapefruit (30 calories) serves two persons. 2 teaspoons of granulated sugar (50 calories) should be added to bring out the flavour of the grapefruit juice.

The juice of one lemon (20 calories) serves two persons. Add about 150 ml ($\frac{1}{4}$ pint) ice-cold water, depending on the size of the lemon used. Add two or three teaspoons of granulated sugar (50–75 calories), but for the slimmer use liquid sweetener.

CANNED FRUIT JUICES

Allow 150 ml ($\frac{1}{4}$ pint) for two servings.

Pineapple juice usually has added sugar and has a calorific value of 80 for the two servings.

Orange and grapefruit juice can be obtained in unsweetened form with 30 calories per portion for the orange and only 20 calories per portion for the grapefruit.

The flavour of tomato juice varies considerably depending on the make and you may find it necessary to add some seasoning. Calories for tomato juice are about 35 for two small servings.

Cans should be chilled in the refrigerator overnight and shaken before opening. Once they have been opened it is advisable to transfer the contents to a screw-topped jar which then can be stored in the door of the refrigerator for 2 or 3 weeks.

ORANGE ELIXIR

Make up enough for four or six and keep in a jug in the refrigerator for a day or two. Whisk up before serving.

Calories: 135

2 medium oranges
½ lemon
1 size 6 egg

1 teaspoon wheatgerm
4 teaspoons sugar

Squeeze the oranges and lemon and put the juice in the liquidizer goblet with the remaining ingredients and generous 150 ml (¼ pint) water. Switch on at medium speed for ½ minute. Drink immediately. *Serves 2.*

FRESH TOMATO JUICE

When tomatoes are in season it makes a change to have home-made juice and the taste bears little relation to the canned or bottled kind. Do not prepare it more than one day ahead unless you are able to freeze the surplus, as stale juice ferments.

Calories: 20–30 (depending on size of serving)

½ kg (1 lb) fresh, ripe tomatoes
½ teaspoon salt
¼ teaspoon sugar

Put all the ingredients into a blender and switch on for 1 minute at top speed. Press through a sieve into a basin, then discard the pulp and pour the juice into glasses. Chill for 30 minutes. If you have a juicing gadget on your electric mixer or food processor, you can produce very low-calorie vegetable juices, using carrots, spinach, cucumber, tomatoes or a combination of these. These would have virtually no calories worth calculating. *Serves 2 to 3.*

2
Lunches and Light Suppers

Lunch and supper dishes can be interchangeable, and whether you have these at lunchtime or at suppertime depends on the job you do. You may be a housewife at home much of the day, which allows you to vary your routine, or an office worker with no access to the kitchen at midday. Another influencing factor is whether you are on a normal slimming diet or having a compensatory low-calorie day, and of course whether you are socializing at midday or in the evening.

Mothers must either save up their calories and eat with the children when they come home from school or stay well away whilst the children are having their meal. This applies particularly if the children go to bed before husbands come home from work. Latecomers should be encouraged to reheat their own meals or temptation could overcome the slimmer's good intentions as cooking smells waft up their nostrils.

Whatever your lifestyle, go shopping after you have eaten. Chocolate bars cunningly displayed at the supermarket exit will sorely tempt you if your stomach is making a fuss.

When it is inconvenient to stop for a meal, keep going on drinks such as low-calorie squash (make it hot for a change), Oxo or Bovril, a low-calorie soup or snackettes. But snackette nibbling, if taken to excess, can quickly top up a calorie bill, and at the end of the day might account for 80 to 100 calories. Although low calorie, carrots, if eaten in vast quantities, can cause staining of the pigment and give your skin an orange tinge.

If you are an office worker who has lived off doughnuts and sausage rolls, it will be very hard for you to watch whilst your colleagues continue to scoff these or great indigestible mouth-watering sandwiches or other goodies. Don't let it get you down. You can be seen to be doing the same, but your sandwiches will be unbuttered thin bread, filled with a small amount of ham, cheese or egg, bolstered up with an inch of salad. Treat yourself to some exotic fruit, such as lychees or strawberries out of season and make them all jealous. You can join your friends at the pub if you wish and order a low-calorie drink and ask for un-buttered sandwiches. Publicans are human too. You may well find that a roll is not necessarily more damaging because it takes so long to chew and is often lower in calories, as it takes the place of two slices of bread. In extreme cases, where lunch is out of the question because the calorific allowance has been considerably abused, you must get away from the office at all costs. Tell the others you have shopping to do and then spend the time in the local department store and treat yourself to a present with the money that you have saved.

Devotees of pre-packaged slimmers' products may find these helpful, but they should be taken with water rather than milk on compensatory days. Slimming aids are confidence tricks, but do have their uses, for they allow the consumer to regulate the diet. The manufacturers state that these aids only succeed as part of a calorie-controlled diet, so you cannot have them and lots of other things too. They are very good as portion controllers and, even if you like the taste, you must limit yourself to your day's calorie intake. Meal replacements are not necessarily low in calories, but do contain all the necessary nutrients. If you are unable to count your own calories, are willing to spend money on meal replacements and are prepared to have this fodder rather than food, you will be receiving a healthy, foolproof diet. The trouble is that three biscuits feel like three biscuits and not a real meal and often the calorie value is the same as ordinary biscuits. Liquid meal replacement, such as is prescribed for invalids, is not very different from slimmers' liquid meal replacement. But are you going to be happy with liquid? Remember we are fat people and are unlikely to be psychologically satisfied this way. And, as for those toffees that are supposed to take the edge off the appetite, they are so delicious that I had eaten a boxful before I even thought of having the recommended drink to bulk me out. Nevertheless there is something to be said for diet chocolate bars. If you replace a meal with one of these, you may feel slightly sick because you are eating a whole bar of chocolate, instantly curing the craving.

Whichever commercial aid you purchase, don't buy special offers in large quantities, because there is always a chance that you won't like them. Television advertisements have a great effect on us, but can be misleading. In fact, commercial television is a bad influence on the slimmer altogether. Advertisements frequently feature food and it always looks so good that it is hard to resist popping into the kitchen for a quick snack.

BAKED BEANS AND TOMATO ON TOAST

When toast is to be topped with a wettish mixture it should first be sparingly buttered. This prevents the liquid in the beans from seeping into the toast, making it soggy.

Calories: 275

142 g (5 oz) can baked
   beans in tomato sauce
1 medium tomato

40 g (1½ oz) slice from
   large white loaf
7 g (¼ oz) low-calorie
   margarine spread

Puncture the can and partially immerse in hot water. Bring to the boil and simmer for 5 minutes. Remove the can and boil the tomato for ½ minute, then drain and slice. Protect the upper hand with a cloth while opening the can. Toast the bread, spread with low-calorie margarine, top with beans and sliced tomato. *Serves 1.*

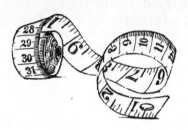

POACHED EGG AND BAKED BEANS ON TOAST

You could manage with less than a whole can of beans, but 142 g (5 oz) is the smallest can available and you will only finish up the beans after lunch unless you are very strong-minded.

Calories: 335

142 g (5 oz) can baked beans in tomato sauce
salt
1 size 6 egg

40 g (1½ oz) slice from large white loaf
7 g (¼ oz) low-calorie margarine spread

Puncture the top of the can and partially immerse in hot water. Bring to the boil and simmer for 5 minutes. Remove carefully, taking care not to scald your hands. Add salt to the water, swirl with the handle of a wooden spoon and break the egg into the whirlpool. Lower the heat and poach for a minute or two. Toast the bread, spread with the low-calorie margarine. Top with the beans. Remove the egg from the pan with a slotted spoon and place on the beans. *Serves 1.*

BEEFBURGER POUCH

There are beefburgers, hamburgers and steaklets produced by various manufacturers and they can also be purchased frozen or canned. However, you can quite easily prepare them at home, buying the very best quality mince. I used Bird's Eye beefburgers in this recipe. You will find that frozen products are increasingly being marked with the calorie value.

Calories: 160

2 beefburgers	1 large firm tomato, halved
1 small onion, sliced in thin rings	1 pitta bread
	$\frac{1}{2}$ teaspoon French mustard

Space out the beefburgers, onion rings and tomato on the grill rack. Preheat the grill and cook thoroughly, turning the beefburgers over once. Push to one side of the rack, putting the pitta on the other. Switch off the heat, turn the pitta over and leave for a few moments to warm through. Mop up any surplus fat from the beefburgers with kitchen paper. Spread mustard over the beefburgers. Cut the pitta in half crosswise and fill each half with a beefburger, onion rings and tomato. Serve hot. *Serves 2.*

CARROT, ORANGE AND COTTAGE CHEESE SALAD

The quantities here will serve two and this salad will keep for a day or two in the refrigerator. In fact you will have two different salads in one, because the flavour changes as the ingredients blend.

Calories per serving: 100

1 crisp lettuce heart
90 g (3½ oz) cottage cheese
2 medium-size juicy oranges
2 large carrots, finely
   grated

2 teaspoons fresh lemon
   juice
¼ teaspoon salt
1/8 teaspoon freshly ground
   black pepper

Shred the lettuce coarsely and arrange in individual wooden bowls. Cover with a mound of cottage cheese. Remove the peel, pith and pips from the oranges and chop the flesh roughly. Mix with the carrots add the lemon juice, salt and pepper. Pile mixture on top of the cottage cheese. Cover until required. *Serves 2.*

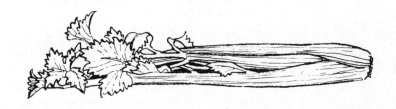

CELERY TOPPERS

Serve as a snackette for two or a low-calorie meal with a cup of hot Bovril.

Calories: 110

1 celery stalk
25 g (1 oz) Edam cheese,
   grated
3 small gherkins, chopped

½ teaspoon made mustard
1 tablespoon natural low-
   fat yogurt

Pare the strings and cut the celery into four even lengths. Combine the other ingredients and pile into the hollows of the celery. *Serves 1.*

CHEESE AND CELERY SOUFFLÉ

Calories: 340

15 g (½ oz) butter
15 g (½ oz) plain flour
150 ml (¼ pint) skimmed
    milk
2 size 2 eggs, separated
75 g (3 oz) Edam cheese,
    grated

2 celery stalks, finely
    chopped
3 drops Tabasco pepper
    sauce
salt
pepper

Melt the butter in a saucepan, stir in the flour and cook over a moderate heat for 1 minute. Away from the heat, gradually stir in the milk. Return to the heat and bring to the boil, stirring all the time. Cook for a further minute, then allow to cool slightly. Add the beaten egg yolks, cheese, celery, Tabasco sauce, salt and pepper. Whisk the egg whites in a grease-free bowl until stiff but not dry. Stir one spoonful of whites into the sauce, then fold in the remainder with a metal spoon. Pour into a greased soufflé dish so that the mixture reaches no higher than three-quarters of the way up. Bake in the centre of a fairly hot oven (190°C, 375°F, Gas 5) for 30 to 35 minutes, but do not open the oven to inspect for the first 20 minutes. Serve at once with a green salad.   *Serves 2.*

Opposite The dessert trolley holds Chilled Coffee Soufflés, page 142, Blackberry and Strawberry Jellies, page 139, Stuffed Oranges, page 151, Fresh Peach and Raspberry Dessert, page 145, and Meringues with French Custard, page 147.

Overleaf Salmon Royale, page 61. A complete dinner party menu of American Grapefruit, page 25, Red-cooked Beef and Cucumber Sheaves, page 83, boiled rice and shrimps, and Japanese Cheesecake, page 146.

Opposite page 177 Granary Open Sandwich, page 182.

CHEESE AND HAM RATATOUILLE

You can prepare the recipe up to the asterisk then finish it off when it is required.

Calories: 140–280 (depending on size of serving)

225 g (8 oz) courgettes, thinly sliced
1 onion, chopped
227 g (8 oz) can tomatoes
1 tablespoon tomato purée
1 tablespoon fresh basil leaves (or 1 teaspoon dried basil)

100 g (4 oz) mushrooms, sliced
25 g (1 oz) ham, chopped
salt
pepper
25 g (1 oz) Edam cheese, grated

Combine the courgettes, onion, tomatoes and their juice, the tomato purée and basil in a saucepan. Cook over gentle heat for 20 to 25 minutes until the courgettes are soft. Stir in the mushrooms and ham and cook for a further 5 minutes. Season with salt and pepper.* Pour into individual flameproof dishes, sprinkle with the cheese and place under a hot grill until the cheese has melted.   *Serves 1 or 2.*

CHICKEN AND CUCUMBER PARCEL

Don't judge this recipe by its appearance, which is rather pale, but by its taste and texture, which 'eats' like fish. The cooking time remains the same regardless of how many parcels are cooked at the same time, but a suitably sized saucepan must be used. To make foil parcels watertight, the edges must be treble-folded. Put the chicken in the middle of a generous piece of foil, fold the sides to the middle, then bring the two ends together over the centre and fold or roll to form a tight seal and a compact parcel.

Calories: 210

175 g (6 oz) boned chicken   salt
  breast   pepper
6 slices cucumber   1 slice lemon

Skin the chicken. Make two deep horizontal slits in the chicken, not quite separating it into slices. Fill each pocket with cucumber slices sprinkled with salt and pepper. Top with the slice of lemon and wrap tightly in foil. Immerse in a pan of simmering water, cover with a lid and cook for $\frac{1}{2}$ hour. Remove the parcel with a slotted spoon and shake off the surplus water. Unwrap on the plate, discarding the lemon slice. *Serves 1.*

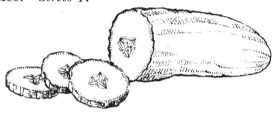

CHICKEN OTTOMAN

Frozen poultry must first be thawed. Leaving aside the bacteria problem, if frozen chicken portions are cooked under fierce heat before they are fully thawed out, they become very tough. This recipe provides an attractive dish which is also good for entertaining when the portions can be baked in a hot oven. There is then no need to turn the pieces over. A rich mushroom and wine sauce could be offered separately.

Calories: 230

175 g (6 oz) boned chicken   2 rings red pepper
  breast   paprika
salt   trace of vegetable oil
pepper
4 button mushrooms, finely
  sliced

Skin the chicken, then season the flesh with salt and pepper. Slash vertically down the centre and open up to form a pocket. Fill with the mushrooms and top with pepper rings and a good sprinkling of paprika. Brush a piece of foil sparingly with oil and place over the peppers. Turn upside down so that the foil is underneath, then brush the chicken with oil. Place chicken in a grill pan and cook for 5 minutes, then turn over, remove the foil and grill the top on medium heat for a further 4 to 5 minutes until the chicken is cooked through. *Serves 1.*

CURRIED EGGS WITH PRAWNS

It is cheaper to buy a large packet of frozen prawns and use a few at a time as required than to buy small packets. Prawns come in different sizes *and* prices, so it is worth spending a little time comparing these.

Calories: 215

2 size 4 eggs, hard-boiled
75 g (3 oz) peeled prawns
½ teaspoon paprika
2 teaspoons cornflour
1 tablespoon curry powder

150 ml (¼ pint) skimmed milk
salt
pepper
25 g (1 oz) Edam cheese

Halve the eggs and arrange them cut side up in a small shallow ovenproof dish. Top each egg with prawns and paprika. Blend the cornflour and curry powder with the milk and bring to the boil, stirring all the time until the sauce thickens. Add salt and pepper to taste. Pour the sauce over the eggs and sprinkle with the cheese. Bake in a moderate oven (180°C, 350°F, Gas 4) for 15 minutes. *Serves 2.*

CURRIED PRAWNS AND RICE

Calories: 170–340 (depending on size of serving)

2 tablespoons raw, long-grain rice
1 small onion, finely chopped
shake of garlic powder
1 tablespoon vegetable oil

1 tablespoon curry powder
75 g (3 oz) frozen peeled prawns
2 medium tomatoes, sliced
salt
pepper

Cook the rice by your usual method and prepare the curry while it is cooking. Fry the onion and garlic powder in the oil until soft. Stir in the curry powder and cook for $\frac{1}{2}$ minute, then stir in the prawns and 5 tablespoons water. Bring to the boil, add the tomatoes, then reduce the heat and simmer uncovered for 10 minutes until the sauce thickens. Season to taste with salt and pepper. Spoon the rice on to plates and pour over the curry. *Serves 1 to 2.*

DEVILLED EGGS

The eggs are poached in a piquant sauce and the quantity of ingredients will serve two. Devilled eggs would be suitable as a starter and the recipe can be doubled with ease. They can either be cooked in a flameproof dish or in the frying pan. If you use a frying pan, there is always the risk of breaking the eggs before you bring them to the table.

Calories: 155–305 (depending on size of serving)

1 small onion
1 small clove garlic
15 g ($\frac{1}{2}$ oz) butter
2 tablespoons tomato purée
1 teaspoon French mustard

pinch mixed herbs
salt
pepper
2 size 5 eggs

Slice the onion thinly and crush the garlic. Sauté gently in the butter until just golden. Stir in the tomato purée, mustard, herbs, salt and pepper. Add 5 or 6 tablespoons water. Cook gently for 4 to 5 minutes, stirring occasionally. Break the eggs separately and slide into the sauce beside one another. Cover and cook until the eggs are just set. *Serves 1 to 2.*

EGG AND ANCHOVY SALAD

To remove excess salt put the anchovies in a saucer of milk and leave for ½ hour before draining.

Calories: 150

1 size 6 egg
2 anchovy fillets, well
    drained
1 lettuce heart

1 small tomato
10 thin slices cucumber
1 tablespoon low-calorie
    salad dressing

Put the egg into cold water, bring to the boil and simmer for 11 minutes. Cool under cold running water, shell and cut into thin slices. Chop the anchovies, shred the lettuce heart and slice the tomato. Mix together and spread on a plate. Arrange alternate egg and cucumber slices on top and spoon the dressing in the centre. *Serves 1.*

FISH ANISE

When entertaining a slimming friend to lunch, serve fresh fish fillet but if you are on your own a frozen fish steak will do. Cook two and have the other cold tomorrow.

Calories: 165

225 ml (7½ fl. oz) skimmed milk
2 teaspoons Pernod
salt
pepper

2 × 100 g (4 oz) fresh fish fillets
1 size 6 egg yolk
½ stick celery, finely chopped

Put the milk and Pernod in a frying pan. Bring to the boil, then lower the heat and simmer for 2 minutes. Season the fish and lay the fillets side by side in the pan. Cover and cook gently for 10 to 15 minutes. Using a slotted spoon transfer the fish to a heated serving dish. Pour the milk and pernod into a bowl, beat in the egg yolk and return to the pan, stirring continuously until the sauce thickens. Pour through a strainer over the fish. Garnish with finely chopped celery. *Serves 2.*

GRANARY OPEN SANDWICH

Calories: 165

25 g (1 oz) slice granary bread
15 g (½ oz) Edam cheese, sliced

1 tablespoon low-calorie salad dressing
25 g (1 oz) peeled prawns

Toast the bread, then cover with the cheese. Spread with the salad dressing and pile the prawns on top. *Serves 1.*

GRILLS

The calorific values for fish are easy to work out but meat contains varying amounts of fat, so use the values as a guide only and add a few more calories to be on the safe side and avoid spoiling your diet. I have included the small quantity of oil or butter needed when grilling and the quantities are for raw weight and for one serving.

	Calories
chicken drumstick	100
chicken joint	200
100 g (4 oz) gammon steak	360
175 g (6 oz) halibut steak including bone	140
100 g (4 oz) herring	200
175 g (6 oz) fillet plaice, haddock or cod	140
2 sheep's kidneys	160
100 g (4 oz) lamb chop, lean part only	310
100 g (4 oz) lamb chop, lean and fat	610
100 g (4 oz) liver, thinly sliced	160
100 g (4 oz) pork chop, lean part only	140
100 g (4 oz) pork chop, with some fat	240
100 g (4 oz) pork chop, whole chop	520
sausages, each	110
100 g (4 oz) steak, fillet	310
100 g (4 oz) steak, rump, with small amount fat	410
100 g (4 oz) veal chop	130
2 × 25 g (1 oz) slices Worscht	150

When grilling steaks for yourself you will know from experience how long to give them. If you are entertaining a slimming friend whose taste may differ, you will need to allow for a 1 in. thick steak 2 minutes per side for '*bleu*', $2\frac{1}{2}$ minutes for rare and 3 to $3\frac{1}{2}$ minutes for medium. A well-done steak takes 8 to 10 minutes in all. If the steaks are thinner, cut these times by half. Use a pastry brush to spread the oil and make it go further, and seal the steaks quickly on both sides under a preheated grill before continuing cooking.

GRAPEFRUIT LUNCH

Calories: 160

1 grapefruit
1 red-skinned apple
25 g (1 oz) piece Edam cheese

Cut the grapefruit in a zigzag design one-third of the way down. Scoop out the flesh and remove the membrane and any pith, but reserve the juice. Quarter, core and slice the apple and dice the cheese. Mix all the ingredients together and replace in the grapefruit shell. Cover with the lid if not being eaten immediately. *Serves 1.*

HOME-MADE CHICKEN SOUP

Provided it is skimmed thoroughly and all fat removed, chicken soup is very low in calories and can be used as a basis for low-calorie meals, snackettes or stock. Shred some of the cooked chicken and add to the soup or use in other dishes. But, to be honest, a chicken will not have much taste after it has been boiling for 4 hours. When the soup is well reduced, it can be frozen as concentrated cubes in ice-box trays. Make up a large quantity of the soup and keep in a cool place, but you should boil it up thoroughly every day until it is used.

Calories: 30 (per bowl)

To make 2–3 l (4 pints) soup you will need:

1 boiling chicken, cut into 8	4 carrots, cut into medium chunks
giblets from the chicken plus any that the butcher will give you	2 onions, quartered
	12 black peppercorns
	salt

Put the chicken and the giblets in the largest saucepan that you have, cover with cold water and bring to the boil. Spoon away the scum and continue boiling and skimming until scum no longer forms. Add the vegetables and peppercorns and season sparingly with salt. Lower the heat, cover and cook gently for 4 hours, topping up with water if necessary. Do not use a pressure cooker as the lengthy cooking time extracts all the flavour. Strain the soup into a large bowl. Pick the meat from the chicken for use in other dishes. Leave the soup to cool, then strain again and chill until the fat rises and sets in a solid layer on the top. Remove this fat and use the soup as required, adjusting seasoning to taste.

Here are three serving suggestions – 300 ml ($\frac{1}{2}$ pint) soup will be reduced to 200 to 250 ml (7 to 8 fl. oz) after cooking, so make sure it is not too salty to begin with. The quantities are for single servings:

Chicken soup with noodles

Calories: 75

300 ml ($\frac{1}{2}$ pint) home-made chicken soup	salt
7 g ($\frac{1}{4}$ oz) noodles	pepper

Bring the soup to the boil, add the noodles and cook until soft. Add seasoning if necessary.

Chicken soup with mushrooms

Calories: 55

300 ml (½ pint) home-made   salt
   chicken soup   pepper
3 mushrooms

Chop the mushrooms and put in a pan with the soup. Bring to the boil, then lower the heat and simmer for 10 minutes to cook the mushrooms. Add seasoning if necessary.

Chicken soup with carrots

Calories: 55

300 ml (½ pint) home-made   salt
   chicken soup   pepper
1 carrot, grated *or* 2 canned
   carrots, sliced

Put the soup and carrots in a saucepan, bring to the boil, then simmer until the carrots are tender. Add seasoning if necessary.

JIFFY ASPARAGUS

Calories: 70

225 g (7·94 oz) can   2 tablespoons skimmed
   asparagus cocktail   milk
   spears   salt
2 teaspoons cornflour   pepper

Tip the contents of the can into a small saucepan and cook until thoroughly heated. Meanwhile blend the cornflour and milk in a fair-sized bowl. Strain the asparagus liquid into the bowl. Put the asparagus on a warm plate and cover to keep hot. Stir the liquid thoroughly, then return to the pan and bring to the boil, stirring continuously until the sauce thickens. Season with salt and pepper, pour the liquid over the asparagus and eat while hot. *Serves 1 very generously.*

LAMB AND SALAD PITTA

Pitta is Arab bread which, when warmed, puffs up and on cutting can be opened up like a pouch. Pitta can conveniently replace bread in sandwiches – the filling is less likely to fall out. Reserve a few marinated lamb cubes prepared for kebabs that you served the night before. Marinating takes several hours, so that it is not worth preparing meat especially for sandwiches this way.

Calories: 290

175 g (6 oz) cubed lamb,   4 fresh onion rings
   marinated   shredded lettuce
1 pitta bread

Remove the rack and preheat the grill. Put the drained lamb cubes into the pan and cook under a hot grill, turning the pieces rapidly so that all sides are sealed. Continue cooking for about 5 minutes, then put the pitta on the rack, replace on the pan and switch off the heat. Turn over after a few moments and cut in half crosswise. Stuff with the lamb, onion rings and lettuce. Best served at once, but can be eaten cold. *Serves 2.*

LEEK AND BACON AU GRATIN

Calories: 190

2 leeks, washed and
trimmed
1 rasher streaky bacon,
rind removed

25 g (1 oz) Edam cheese,
grated
1 tomato, sliced

Cut the leeks into 1 in. lengths and cook in boiling salted water for 10 minutes until just cooked. Meanwhile grill the bacon well and drain on kitchen paper. Drain the leeks and arrange in a flameproof dish. Sprinkle with the cheese, cover with tomato slices and place under the hot grill until the cheese has melted. Crumble the bacon on top and serve at once. *Serves 1.*

LIVER AND TOMATO SLAW

Calories: 240

100 g (4 oz) lamb's liver,
trimmed and sliced
½ teaspoon vegetable oil
salt
pepper
1 tomato, halved
small piece white cabbage,
finely shredded
1 small onion, finely
chopped

1 small carrot, grated
2 tablespoons natural, low-
fat yogurt
1 teaspoon low-calorie
salad dressing
1 teaspoon horseradish
sauce
1 tablespoon freshly
chopped parsley

Brush the liver with oil and season with salt and pepper. Grill on both sides until you see little red bubbles on top. Grill the tomato halves at the same time, meanwhile combine all the other ingredients. Serve the slaw as a side salad with the liver and tomato. *Serves 1.*

MARROW BOATS

Mince loses about half of its calories when fried in its own fat and well drained. The recipe serves two, but could be prepared up to the 'filling stage' and stored in the refrigerator for 24 hours, enabling you to cook half one day and half the next if you are eating alone. Serve with grilled tomatoes.

Calories: 255

225 g (8 oz) lean minced beef

1 small onion, finely chopped

1 tablespoon tomato purée

$\frac{1}{4}$ teaspoon Worcestershire sauce

$\frac{1}{2}$ teaspoon mixed dried herbs

$\frac{1}{4}$ teaspoon Bovril (undiluted)

1 tablespoon flour

salt

pepper

1 small marrow

Break the meat into a frying pan and cook over medium heat until the fat oozes out. Add the onion, raise the heat and cook until brown. Drain away the fat. Stir in the tomato purée, Worcestershire sauce, herbs, Bovril and water. Simmer for 20 minutes. Blend the flour with a few tablespoons cold water, stir into the meat mixture and bring to the boil. Season to taste when the mixture thickens. Peel the marrow, cut in half lengthwise and scoop out the seeds. Boil in a large saucepan of salted water until just tender. Drain carefully on kitchen paper until both sides are dry. Lay the marrow halves hollows upwards side by side in an ovenproof casserole. Fill with the meat mixture, cover tightly and bake in a fairly hot oven (190°C, 375°F, Gas 5) for 20 to 30 minutes. *Serves 2.*

PARSEE CHICKEN

Chicken is easy to obtain. You can either buy a whole chicken and joint it yourself, or buy chicken portions, frozen, fresh-chilled or freshly cut. Of course, poultry must be completely thawed before cooking and you can hasten the process with the discreet use of cold water. Sometimes it is better to cook chicken before skinning, but in any case don't eat the skin because it is very fatty and these are calories you can do without. This recipe is versatile and, provided you follow the preparation directions, you can easily vary the flavourings, adding a little more or less as you wish. Be sure to grate the onion finely. You can use a liquidizer or crush in small pieces with a garlic press. Tandoori powder is available at most Indian-style grocers, but you could substitute a mixture of turmeric, ginger, paprika and curry powder. Double up this recipe as many times as you like, but allow a little longer cooking time. This is delicious hot or cold. Serve with an onion and tomato salad.

Calories: 200

250 g (9 oz) chicken joint
1 small onion, finely grated

1 tablespoon natural, low-fat yogurt
1 tablespoon tandoori powder

Skin the chicken and slash deeply in two or three places. Mix the onion with the yogurt and tandoori powder. Rub into the chicken thoroughly, then cover the chicken and put it in the refrigerator for at least 4 hours. Remove the rack and put the chicken in the grill pan. Grill under medium heat, turning over once during cooking, and baste with the pan juices. When cooked the chicken should be a glowing golden colour. *Serves 1.*

PORK AND CUCUMBER TOPPER

The simplest way to use up a joint is to have it cold. So perhaps this should be called Monday's Pork.

Calories: 150

shredded lettuce
40 g (1½ oz) slice lean
  roast pork
1 tablespoon natural, low-
  fat yogurt
1 teaspoon chopped chives

pinch dry mustard
pinch celery salt
pepper
few drops lemon juice
2 in. chunk cucumber, cut
  into matchstick strips

Arrange a bed of lettuce on a plate. Cover with the pork. Combine the yogurt, chives, mustard, celery salt, pepper and lemon juice. Mix in the cucumber and pile on top of the slice of pork. *Serves 1.*

SALAD NIÇOISE

Serve this salad with as much lettuce as you like.

Calories: 200

1 rollmop herring
1 tomato, skinned
1 size 5 egg, hard boiled
1 small onion, sliced into
  thin rings

8 whole green snap beans,
  cooked
2 tablespoons natural, low-
  fat yogurt
fresh ground black pepper

Slice the herring into thin strips. Cut the tomato into eight and quarter the hard-boiled egg. Mix in a wooden bowl with the onion rings and the whole beans. Add the yogurt and pepper and toss thoroughly. Serve with shredded lettuce. *Serves 1.*

SALMON AND MUSHROOM CREAMS

Serve with half a slice of toast or a crispbread if you have calories to spare.

Calories: 175

99 g (3½ oz) can salmon
100 g (4 oz) mushrooms,
   sliced
7 g (¼ oz) butter

156 g (5½ oz) can
   condensed cream of
   mushroom soup

Drain and flake the salmon, removing any bones. Put the mushrooms and butter in a non-stick pan, stirring over moderate heat until soft. Add the salmon and soup and heat thoroughly. Pour into individual dishes.   *Serves 2.*

SCRAMBLED EGGS AND TOMATOES

Have a couple of bran biscuits (50 calories per oz) with this supper dish. They are crisp, crunchy and really filling. If you have found your new diet somewhat constipating, the bulky bran will put this right. Both Waitrose and Marks and Spencer sell them.

Calories: 240

3 medium tomatoes
pinch celery salt
15 g (½ oz) low-calorie
   margarine spread
2 size 5 eggs

2 tablespoons skimmed
   milk
salt
pepper

Chop the tomatoes roughly, put in a non-stick pan with the celery salt and half the spread. Sauté gently for 5 minutes until soft. Remove the tomatoes and keep hot. Beat the eggs with the milk, salt and pepper. Pour into the pan, add the remaining spread and cook over a moderate heat, stirring continuously, until only just set. Add the tomatoes, stir briefly, then serve at once. *Serves 1.*

SLIMMER'S QUICHE

Starch-reduced bread has 35 calories in a slice and, while not being any more filling than a half-slice from a small white loaf, it will look more on a plate. Starch-reduced bread is used here instead of the forbidden pastry crust.

Calories: 245

2 slices Nimble or Slimcea bread
2 size 3 eggs
4 tablespoons skimmed milk
25 g (1 oz) ham, chopped
1 tablespoon frozen peas

2 tomatoes, skinned and sliced
40 g (1½ oz) Edam cheese, grated
1 onion, chopped
salt
pepper

Cut the bread into quarters and use to line the sides of a small pie dish. Beat the eggs and milk together, then stir in the ham, peas, tomatoes, cheese and onion. Season with salt and pepper and pour the mixture into the prepared dish. Bake in a moderate oven (180°C, 350°F, Gas 4) for 30 to 40 minutes. *Serves 2.*

SOUFFLÉ OMELETTE

Eggs are a protein food often used by vegetarians to replace meat and fish. Apart from their food value, the plus factor is that they are quick and easy to cook. This soufflé omelette, being puffed up with air, makes the meal seem so much bigger.

Calories: 260

2 size 5 eggs, separated   pepper
1 tablespoon skimmed milk   15 g ($\frac{1}{2}$ oz) butter
salt

Preheat a medium grill. Beat the egg yolks with the milk, salt and pepper. Using clean beaters, whisk the whites until stiff, then fold them into the yolks. Melt the butter in a non-stick pan, pour the eggs into the pan and cook over a moderate heat for 2 to 3 minutes until set and brown underneath. Put under the grill and cook for about 5 minutes until set and golden brown. *Serves 1*.

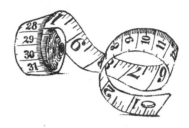

SPINACH AND EGG CASSEROLE

Calories : 290

3 size 6 eggs   50 g (2 oz) Edam cheese,
227 g (8 oz) packet frozen   grated
    chopped spinach   3 tablespoons skimmed
ground nutmeg   milk
salt   2 tomatoes
pepper

Hard boil and slice the eggs. Cook the spinach according to the directions on the packet and season with nutmeg, salt and pepper. Arrange layers of spinach and egg and half the cheese in a small casserole dish. Pour the milk over the layers, then top with the remaining cheese and bake in a moderate oven (180°C, 350°F, Gas 4) for 10 to 15 minutes, until the mixture is well heated and the cheese has melted. Bake the tomatoes in a separate dish or cook under the grill and serve with the casserole. *Serves 2*.

STUFFED JACKET POTATOES

A stuffed jacket potato makes a satisfying meal, but because it is so appetizing you must not put temptation in your way. It would be no good telling you to split the cooked potato and just eat one half, because you might not have the will-power to resist eating it all. The answer here is to bake a smaller potato and eat it all. Potatoes are not colossally high in calorific value (raw potatoes have 25 calories per ounce) but they always seem to be, as they are often pre-pared with fat or because helpings are unnecessarily large. The average baking potato weighs 200 g (7 oz). Choose and *weigh* a 175 g (6 oz) potato and save 25 calories. If you prefer a soft-skinned potato, wrap in foil before baking.

Calories: 150 (without filling)

175 g (6 oz) waxy old potato

Scrub the potato but do not break the skin. Dry, prick all over and bake directly on the middle shelf of a fairly hot oven (200°C, 400°F, Gas 6) for 45 minutes to 1 hour until soft when pressed. Leave the oven on, but remove the potato and leave it to cool for a few minutes, then cut in half lengthwise. Scoop out the pulp without breaking the skin, mix with the filling (see below) and pile back into the skin. Put on a non-stick tray and reheat in the oven for 10 to 15 minutes; there should be heat left for this. *Serves 1.*

Cheese and pineapple filling

Calories: 110

50 g (2 oz) slice fresh – or. defrosted – pineapple
50 g (2 oz) curd cheese

1 teaspoon freshly chopped parsley
salt
pepper

Chop the pineapple and mix with the remaining ingredients (and the potato pulp). *Serves 1.*

Ham and orange filling

Calories: 120

25 g (1 oz) lean, trimmed
    cooked ham
1 teaspoon butter
2 teaspoons fresh orange
    juice

2 teaspoons natural, low-
    fat yogurt
1 teaspoon egg yolk
salt
pepper

Chop the ham finely and mix with the remaining ingredients (and the potato pulp). *Serves 1.*

QUICK LOW-CALORIE DESSERTS

Many of the quick desserts listed below are pieces of fresh fruit, and the riper they are, the higher the calorific value, because more natural sugar has developed in them. Yogurts vary according to the make. Home-made yogurt (made from skimmed milk) will have the same value as the milk itself (5 fl. oz=50 calories). When made from whole milk, the same size has 100 calories. Commercial brands are available in varying sizes and may be low-fat, made from skimmed milk only, or have a fruit content, and some are sweetened. A 142 ml (5 fl. oz) carton of fruit-flavoured yogurt has about 150 calories, as there are 30 calories per fluid ounce.

	Calories per serving
1 dessert apple	40
1 small banana	65
1 medium orange	40
1 satsuma	20
1 pear	40
½ grapefruit	15
12 grapes	35

100 g (4 oz) raspberries	20
100 g (4 oz) blackberries	40
198 g (7 oz) can fruit in water:	
apricots	25
pineapple	40
pears	40
peaches	40
fruit salad	40
2 canned peach halves, drained	75
3 canned apricot halves, drained	75
1 canned pear half, drained	40
1 small individual vanilla ice cream	75
2 ice cream wafers	10
1 packet jelly (made up to 1 pint with hot water serves 4)	95
100 g (4 oz) stewed apple without sugar	40
150 ml ($\frac{1}{4}$ pint) custard made with skimmed milk without sugar	80
150 ml ($\frac{1}{4}$ pint) blancmange made with skimmed milk without sugar	90
150 ml (5 fl. oz) home-made skimmed milk yogurt	50
142 ml (5 fl. oz) average carton purchased natural, low-fat yogurt	75
142 ml (5 fl. oz) average carton purchased, fruit yogurt	150
1 tablespoon single cream	35
1 tablespoon double cream	65
1 tablespoon canned cream	35
1 tablespoon imitation cream	55
1 teaspoon sugar	25
liquid sweetener	nil

I am a chocolate addict, so I cannot allow myself to eat just one chocolate, I have to finish the box. Perhaps you have heard that story before. If you are not passionately fond of confectionery, you will be able to ration yourself. Here are a few often sought-after sweetmeats:

1 Mint Crisp – 25 g (1 oz, 140 calories)	30
1 After Eight Mint – 25 g (1 oz, 120 calories)	35
1 average boiled sweet	20
1 liqueur chocolate	50
4 small squares plain chocolate	65
28·5 g (1 oz) tube fruit gums	70
1 chocolate mallow	75
1 milk chocolate flake	95
1 small Crunchie	90
25 g (1 oz) wine gums	95
28·5 g (1 oz) tube Smarties	130
1 walnut whip	140
1 smallest size bar milk chocolate	180
1 Mars bar (usual size)	270
1 50 g (2 oz) bar Aero	300
1 smallest bar Roasted Almond Plain Chocolate	555

3
Suggested Foods to Take the Edge Off the Appetite before Going Out

Food can be an appetite depressant if eaten at a suitable time before going out to dine or, for that matter, eating at home. It is no good arriving at your hostess' feeling ravenously hungry and throwing caution to the winds, grabbing great quantities of salted peanuts, cheesy biscuits or twiglets (5 calories each). Then, as that guilty feeling descends, your enjoyment of the meal disappears. The struggling dieter is often witnessed gobbling up the roll with lashings of butter (195 calories) before the first course is served or surreptitiously crunching gristicks which, although only 15 calories each, always come wrapped in a cellophane packet with seven or eight alluring friends.

The idea of the following snacklet suggestions is to prevent ominous stomach rumblings, so you can sit righteously staring those tempting nibbles straight in the eye and knowing that you don't need any of them, because you have already eaten your appetizer at home. It is up to you to choose a sweet or savoury item. Often it is best not to indulge in one you are too fond of, to avoid turning your snackette into snacklets. Always accompany the dry items with a hot drink and don't eat them in the kitchen standing up, reading the newspaper at the same time. Sit down, relax and enjoy them.

	Calories to the
Sweet	*nearest 5*
whole grapefruit	30
apple	40
orange	40
225 g (8 oz) strawberries or raspberries	40
Petit Suisse sweetened with liquid sweetener	65
small tub natural, low-fat yogurt	75
150 ml ($\frac{1}{4}$ pint) fruit jelly	95

Savoury

glass cold water	0
Bovril drink	5
4 celery sticks	20
100 g (4 oz) peeled carrots	20
home-made chicken broth (7 fl. oz)	30
crispbread spread with $\frac{1}{4}$ oz paste	30
crispbread with thin spreading of curd cheese and 15 g ($\frac{1}{2}$ oz) lean ham	50
can of low-calorie soup	50–70
crispbread topped with $\frac{1}{2}$ oz Edam cheese, grilled	65
small hard-boiled egg	70
225 g (8 oz) unshelled prawns	80
75 g (3 oz) corn cob	85
90 g ($3\frac{1}{2}$ oz) grilled drumstick	90

PART THREE

Facts and Figures

Eating Out

Dinner at a private house, or indeed any special function – club dinner, wedding or ladies' night – is usually a set meal and the best you can do is to abide by the following basic recommendations. Leave the bread, take small portions of potatoes or rice, say no thank you to cream and choose your drinks carefully. A drinks list will be found on page 230. It is easy to ask for a small tonic water or a tomato juice when an aperitif is offered, but the refusal of table wine is quite another matter. Basically you have to decide either that you drink or that you don't. Funnily enough, you can get away with abstinence if you are female, but the male will be expected to imbibe, unless he says quite categorically that he daren't drink and drive. You will not be able to stop at one, as hosts have an uncanny ability to top up your glass while you are looking the other way, thus you may think you've had one, when in reality it is four. If you decide to drink, choose a dry, rather than a sweet, wine – a sweet wine is almost one-third higher calorie rated.

The above advice also applies when eating out at a restaurant. Here you will be able to select from a menu and the ultimate choice of dish rests fairly and squarely on your own shoulders. An in-depth knowledge of calorific values will come in very useful, although no one can be expected to know how much of which ingredient is in any one dish. This apart, remember you have little control over starter and main course portion sizes. Having overcome the aperitif problem, there may be a dish of *crudités* (raw vegetables), gherkins, olives, peanuts or gristicks actually on the table.

You may pick at the vegetables (no dipping in the sauce) and gherkins.

If you are eating out, enjoy the food but don't spite the diet by choosing high-calorie dishes. If there are two you like equally, choose the one with fewer calories – for example, grilled sole rather than scampi. Scampi are not fattening in themselves, but they treble in calorie value when crumbed and deep fried. Any deep-fried food is out, but the smaller the pieces, the more disastrously fattening they are, since more surfaces come into contact with both crumbs and oil. Home deep frying has the edge on the restaurant style, because at home you are able to use the thinner oils which require high-temperature frying, and the higher the temperature, the quicker the food seals, consequently absorbing less oil. When large quantities are immersed at the same time, the oil cools, causing more fat penetration. But take care, for coated, deep-fried fish may be less fattening than the low-calorie sea food smothered in a delicious cream sauce. It is impossible to work out the calorie content by just looking at a sauce. However, it is helpful to know what the basic sauces contain, so I have listed these below:

Hollandaise Sauce – usually served with artichokes or asparagus.

| 175 g (6 oz) butter | 70 ml (4 tablespoons): |
| 3 egg yolks | *380 calories* |

Béarnaise Sauce – slightly more piquant than Hollandaise and better for the slimmer since the proportion of eggs to butter is higher.

| 100 g (4 oz) butter | 70 ml (4 tablespoons): |
| 2 egg yolks | *260 calories* |

Mayonnaise – served cold. The portions are smaller than for the other sauces, but, as the oil content is higher, this is not reflected in the calorie count.

150 ml ($\frac{1}{4}$ pint) olive oil   70 ml (4 tablespoons):
1 egg yolk   *490 calories*

Remoulade – a mayonnaise flavoured with mustard. It has a similar calorific value to plain mayonnaise.

Tartare – although this sauce is mayonnaise based, cream is often added, making it an unwanted luxury for the slimmer. If you must have something to accompany a fish dish, ask for mayonnaise.

French Dressing – has three or four times as much oil as vinegar. An average portion will be 2 tablespoons.
175–200 calories

White Sauces – have a far lower calorie count than the other sauces. A coating sauce will be based on:

25 g (1 oz) butter   70 ml (4 tablespoons):
25 g (1 oz) flour   *130 calories*
300 ml ($\frac{1}{2}$ pint) milk

Parsley, Caper and Onion Sauces – have the same calorie count as white sauces, but a *Cheese Sauce* has a higher count.
70 ml (4 tablespoons):
190 calories

However, beware, because a restaurant may add to an innocent white sauce a few egg yolks and some cream so, if it's called a cream sauce, it is not for the slimmer.

Brown Sauces – are all based on an Espagnole Sauce (see below) with other ingredients added afterwards

Espagnole Sauce – bacon, butter, flour, tomato paste, vegetables. *70 calories* per waiter's spoonful

Bordelaise Sauce – as Espagnole, but with red wine and more butter. *120 calories* per waiter's spoonful

Gravies – are much less rich than sauces but their calorie content is difficult to calculate. They will probably come out at *20 calories* per tablespoon

Choose items that you don't normally have at home and you will feel you are wallowing in luxury. Lobster, crawfish tails and oysters are frequently served unembellished. As a starter, six oysters will cost the earth in cash, but only 30 calories. Melon, grapefruit and orange cocktail may be boring, but will enable you to go to town on the main course. Asparagus has 50 calories for ten spears, and globe artichokes are 15 calories each. Artichokes are very good because they take a long time to eat, so you don't find yourself nibbling at the rolls whilst the others are still working their way through the first course. But . . . refuse the butter sauce, which will have at least an ounce of butter (226 calories). Half an avocado (100 calories) shoots up astronomically when piled high with prawns and mayonnaise or smothered in vinaigrette. Leave some of the sauce on the plate. Prawn cocktail without the avocado will be 190 calories. Forget paté (110 calories an ounce), as the serving is usually 3 oz plus the Melba toast and butter. You get four thin triangles of this toast for 100 calories, but that would not be nearly enough to go with this quantity of paté. Mixed hors d'oeuvres are misleading, because the meats look so dry, but salami is 100 calories an ounce, the sardine 50 calories and potato salad is full of mayonnaise (42 calories for a level tablespoon) so this starter may set you back 400 to 500 calories. Mediterranean prawns, although fiddly to shell, are low rated and therefore a good choice.

The lowest calorie soup is consommé (50 calories), and all clear soups are preferable to the thick variety. French onion soup has a base of sautéed onions and is served with bread croutes and cheese, and minestrone is also served with cheese. If you decide to spend the 250 calories on the soup, you may as well accept a spoonful of the cheese, which is only 30 calories more. Cream soups are just what they say, soups based on a white sauce with added cream, and you should calculate 300 to 450 calories for a full plate. Lobster bisque is absolutely delicious and comes into this category.

Following on the bisque, if you have a grilled half-lobster as a main course, this is only 140 calories. At the other end of the spectrum is Chicken Kiev – the breast of chicken stuffed with solid butter, then crumbed and deep fried. The head waiter should be able to tell you exactly what each dish is made of, although often nowadays the description is printed in the menu.

Vegetable portions are easily controlled, provided you are concentrating on the waiter while he is serving and not on the conversation. No offence will be taken when the potatoes are declined but, if you really yearn for them, choose boiled, particularly mouth-watering when new. Six chips alone are 100 calories. Sautéed potatoes are swathed in butter and oil and one roast potato is 110 calories. Jacket potatoes are quite good if you are prepared to leave some and omit the butter or soured cream dressing. An average 7 oz potato is 175 calories.

Vegetables such as cauliflower may be dressed with a sauce or arrive on a stainless steel dish in melted butter. Stop the waiter before he ladles the sauce on to your plate. Puréed or mashed vegetables are sure to have hidden butter or cream. Request a dry salad or one with just a trace of dressing. Green salads are frequently drowned in oil and vinegar and served in an accompanying wooden bowl. After a few minutes the dressing starts to sink to the bottom of the bowl, so wait before serving yourself. Lift the salad from the bowl, giving it a surreptitious shake, before transferring it to your plate. A list of vegetables, showing which have the lowest calories, is given on page 228.

Some dessert trollies are loaded with exciting-looking goodies. If you are eating out in the evening, you may be able to put yourself off by the thought of all that exposed, high health risk cream which has been open to germs, sneezes and dust since opening time. When you succumb, for preference choose fresh fruit such as a piece of pineapple, fresh raspberries, strawberries or a peach. Canned fruit should be well drained, so that you will not have to eat the syrup. Other choices are fruit jelly or a small ice cream, and meringue surprisingly enough contains no fat and can have as few as 100 calories. Crème caramel (140 calories) is permitted, but not its cream-and-sugar-soaked sister crème brulée. Profiteroles have 415 calories in an average portion and treacle tart with syrup and breadcrumbs is 310 calories for a modest 3 oz portion. Pastry is out but, if all else fails and you can't resist it, choose shortcrust (half the quantity of fat to flour) and not puff (equal quantities of fat and flour). The calorie count will be much higher when the filling is included. Anyway, don't eat the bit of crust that stands up at the end. Desserts cooked at the table will be loaded with butter and liqueur and aren't really worth the money anyway.

You may be a savoury person and decide to finish with just a tiny, tiny piece of cheese. A good cheese board, groaning with cheeses from near and far, will be irresistible. The just-a-little will turn into just-a-little of two or three and, should the dry biscuits be left within reach, you will need all your will-power to resist. The only time that you can risk the cheese is in a steak house or a more mundane place, where there is strict portion control. You will be served a ration of cheese and wrapped butter, and the waiter will hold tenaciously on to the biscuit basket, shaming you into taking no more than two.

Dining out doesn't always mean eating in the most exclusive restaurants. Not many of us can afford it nowadays. The bistros and ethnic eating houses provide cheaper food and can be just as much fun. The slimmer knows she can have steak and salad wherever she goes, but it is better to choose specialist food in specialist restaurants. Chinese is less fattening than Indian and, in either, choose boiled rather than fried rice. If you are a curry addict, don't ask for a poppadum. Thin they may be, but they are fried. Choose dry vegetable curries or tandoori chicken, which is spiced and baked, but, if you delight in the sauces, briskly paddle the side of the serving spoon on the surface and dish up quickly, as the fatty layer glides away. At the Greek taverna have kebabs only. The moussaka contains fried aubergine, and the stews, such as *stifados*, tend to be steeped in olive oil. Taramasalata has 315 calories per portion and pitta 125 calories each. On no account are you allowed honey-drenched *baclava*, *kataifi* and custard tarts. If you really must end your meal with something sweet, you can have Turkish coffee, loaded with four tea-spoons of sugar for 100 calories.

WHAT ON EARTH DOES IT MEAN?

Interpreting a menu can be confusing: there are traditionally descriptive names for dishes and many that are invented – often named after the establishment. Below is a shortlist of those commonly found on menus. Those marked with an asterisk are high-calorie dishes.

European

Antipasti: Hors d'oeuvres. Italian starter. Includes mixed salami, ham, olives, oil and vinegar dressing, fish, eggs and vegetables.

Avgolemono: Clear chicken soup, garnished with beaten egg and lemon juice.

Beef Stroganoff: Strips of fillet steak cooked with wine and cream, served on a bed of rice.

Bigarade: Orange sauce, usually served with duck. Has some flour, butter and sugar, but not excessive amounts.

Bolognese: Minced meat and tomato sauce, usually served with spaghetti – its value for the slimmer depends on how fatty the mince is.

Bonne Femme: Cooked with white wine and mushrooms.

Bordelaise: Garnished with a red wine and mushroom sauce, based on espagnole sauce.

Bouillabaisse: Thick fish soup containing a mixture of shellfish and white fish.

Bourguignon: Casserole of beef with red wine – not to be confused with Fondu Bourguignon which is chunks of raw beef deep fried at the table by the guest.

Cacciatora: Casserole of poultry or game, browned; then onion, garlic, herbs, tomato and stock and wine are added and simmered slowly.

Calamari/Kalmarika: Baby octopus, squid or inkfish. Low calorie except when deep fried. Ask the waiter.

Carbonnade: Casserole of beef with beer.

Cervelles: Brains. Low calorie except when fried.

Chasseur: Brown sauce flavoured with brandy and mushrooms. As espagnole – white wine and butter extra.

Châteaubriand: Grilled whole fillet of beef, usually served for two and sliced at the table. Sauce served separately. Calories depend on how much you eat.

Colbert: Deep-fried fish with herbed butter tucked inside.

Contrefilet: Roast fillet of beef, usually rare.

Coq au Vin: Chicken casserole, button onions and mushrooms, diced breast pork/bacon, butter, bouquet garni. Flambéed with brandy, red wine and a little flour.

Coquilles St Jacques: Scallops garnished with a cheese sauce, butter, flour, milk.

Cordon Bleu: Veal escalope sandwiched with ham and cheese, crumbed and deep fried.

Croquette Potatoes: Creamed, crumbed and deep fried.

Escalope: Large, thin slice of veal.

*Escargots: Snails with garlic butter and French bread.

Espagnole: Good quality basic brown sauce containing bacon, carrots, onions, tomatoes, tomato purée and mushrooms.

Fegato: Liver.

*Filet de Boeuf Wellington: Whole fillet of beef baked in a pastry case.

Florentine: Served with spinach.

Fricassée: Meat cooked in a thick white sauce.

*Fritto Misto di Mare: Mixed fried sea food.

Fruits de Mer: Mixture of shellfish. There may be an accompanying sauce.

Gazpacho: Cold puréed fresh tomatoes and onions, garnished with peppers, cucumber and a dash of Tabasco pepper sauce. Olive oil.

*Goujons: Strips of white fish, crumbed and deep fried.

Huîtres: Oysters.

*Hummus: Puréed chickpeas with sesame paste and lemon juice.

Italienne: Cooked in a tomato sauce. Butter parsley, white wine and white sauce.

Kebab: Small pieces of marinated meat speared on a skewer and grilled. Sometimes vegetables are included.

*Kiev: Breast of chicken filled with butter, crumbed and deep fried.

Lobster Thermidor: Lobster diced and cooked in a white wine sauce, put back in the shell and browned under the grill.

*Lyonnaise: Sautéed potatoes with onions.

Mange-tout: Young peas cooked in the pod.

Manzo: Beef.

Marengo: Veal or poultry sautéed in oil, then casseroled with white wine, tomato, garlic, mushrooms and sometimes garnished with a fried egg.

Médaillons: Small thin slices of meat. Nearly always in creamy brown sauce.

Meunière: Shallow fried in butter.

Mezes: A selection of stuffed vine leaves, hummus and grilled aubergine with a salad.

Minestrone: Vegetable soup, sometimes containing pasta, garnished with Parmesan cheese.

Mornay: A cheese sauce. Butter, flour, milk and cheese.

Moules Marinière: Mussels stewed and served in the liquid.

Mantaise: Meat cooked in a thick gravy, with turnips, peas and mashed potatoes.

Napolitana: Fresh tomato sauce made with olive oil, usually served with spaghetti.

Osso Bucco: Braised knuckle of veal. Includes beef marrow which is high in calories.

Paysanne: Cooked in simple peasant style, with vegetables braised in butter.

Pizzaiola: Served with chopped tomato, capers with a white wine and garlic sauce.

Portugaise: Cooked in oil, onion and tomato, with some espagnole sauce.

Principessa: Breast of chicken in cream and mushroom sauce.

Prosciutto: Parma ham.

Provençale: Cooked in oil with garlic and tomatoes.

Riz de Veau: Sweetbreads. Ask if they're fried – if so, *we're afraid.

Rognons: Kidneys. Ask how they are cooked.

Saltimbocca: Escalope of veal with Parma ham and herbs in white wine, rolled up and browned in butter.

Scallopine: Small, thin slices of veal.

Steak Diane: Thin steak, fried in butter with Worcestershire sauce, onions and brandy.

Steak au Poivre: Flamed in cognac so that the alcohol evaporates, served in pan juices and with green peppercorns. Sometimes cream is included – ask the waiter.

Steak Tartare: Raw minced beef, bound with onions and raw egg.

Suprème: Boned breast of chicken.

Syllabub: White wine and lemon juice beaten up with cream.

Taramasalata: Cod's roe blended with onion, lemon juice, olive oil and bread.

Tournedos: Thick fillet steak.

Tournedos Rossini: Served with paté and a croûte of bread.

Vapeur: Boiled or steamed new potatoes.

Véronique: Garnished with white sauce and grapes. Sauce enriched with egg yolks.

Vitello Tonnato: Cold veal and tuna fish sauce.

Zabaglione: Frothy sauce made from eggs and Marsala.

Indian

(All curry sauces are based on ghee or oil but these can be avoided by careful dishing up.)

Bhaggi or Baji: Vegetable dishes served dry.

Bhuna: Gently spiced curry.

Biriani: A very rich pilau.

Bombay Duck: Dried fish.

Chapatti: Unleavened thin pancake made of wholemeal flour cooked mainly dry on a griddle.

Dhal: Lentil purée, 25 calories to the ounce.

Dhansak: Slightly 'sweet and sour' curry.

Keema: Minced meat.

Kofta: Minced meat or vegetable balls.

Korma: Medium curry cooked with yogurt.

Madras: Hot curry.

Nan: Heart-shaped form of leavened bread. Rather large and moreish.

Poppadom: Crisp, spiced cracker – fried in oil.

Paratha: Shallow-fried chappatis, buttered.

Pilaff/Pilau: Rice based, cooked in ghee, heavily spiced and containing various named ingredients, e.g. chicken.

Puri: 4 in. flat wholemeal cake, deep fried in oil.

Samosa: Stuffed pastry.

Tandoori: Barbecued and baked in a clay oven.

Tikki: Savoury meat or vegetable cutlet, sometimes fried.

Vindaloo: South Indian hot curry, usually served with potatoes and slightly sour.

Chinese

Bird's Nest Soup: Clear soup literally made from bird's nests.

Chop Suey: Stewed pieces of chicken and ham with vegetables in a soy sauce.

Chow Mein: Strips of vegetables and meat topped with fried crispy noodles.

Fuyong: Fried meat or vegetables topped with a firm omelette.

AVERAGE RESTAURANT PORTIONS CALORIE CHART

It is impossible to judge exactly how many calories there are in dishes frequently appearing on restaurant menus, but here is a rough guide to the nearest 50 for easy calculation.

Starters and soups

Artichoke (with butter)	250	Minestrone	250
Avocado Vinaigrette	250	Mixed Hors d'Oeuvres	450
Asparagus (with butter)	250	Moules Marinière	200
Cannelloni	450	Oysters (6)	50
Chicken Liver Paté		Rich Paté (with toast	
(with toast and butter)	400	and butter)	600
Consommé	50	Prawn Cocktail	200
Cream of Tomato Soup	300	Smoked Salmon (with	
French Onion Soup	250	brown bread and	
Grapefruit (half)	15	butter)	350
Lobster Bisque	400	Smoked Trout (with	
Melon (without added	50	horseradish sauce)	200
sugar)	50	Whitebait	300

Main courses

Beef Strogonoff (plus rice)	650	Grilled Steak (depending on size – usually 7 oz)	350
Chicken Tandoori	250	Sole Véronique	350
Coq au Vin	650	Veal Cordon Bleu	650
Filet de Boeuf Wellington (including sauce)	1050	Veal Marsala	400
		Vitello Tonnato	500
Grilled Lobster	150		

Desserts

Apple Pie	300	Coupe Jacques	250
Black Forest Gâteau	250	Fruit Salad	200
Cheesecake	250	Green Figs in Syrup	100
Crème Caramel	150	Lemon Meringue Pie	200
Crêpes Suzette	250		

Do not order any of the following as they all have over 300 calories:

Baked Jam Roll
Bakewell Tart
Christmas Pudding
Cornish Pasty
Danish Pastries
Individual Pork Pie
Jam Doughnuts
Marron Mont Blanc
Mincemeat Tart

Profiteroles
Rum Baba
Sherry Trifle
Spotted Dick
Steak and Kidney Pudding or Pie
Syrup Sponge
Treacle Tart

The Tools of the Trade

You will recall that you have to cut down by 3500 calories to lose $\frac{1}{2}$ kg (1 lb) of body weight. Do this over a one-week period and don't let it drag on over ten days or you will lose count. Work out your total weekly calorie allowance and then divide it up to suit your diary.

The sociable slimmer may lose only $\frac{1}{2}$ kg (1 lb) a week but this diet plan is guaranteed to work. You can have one weekly binge on the 1000 calories' diet but, if you cut down to 750 calories, you may eat almost anything you like on an entertainment meal. Save up your calories before you go rather than compensating afterwards, otherwise you may find that you have left yourself with only 50 calories to last until the end of the week. On a non-sociable week stick to 1000 calories a day to boost the weight loss.

To calorie count successfully you must write down everything you consume. First invest in a pad of paper which will not easily get thrown away. One whole week before you start serious dieting, write down every vestige of food that passes your lips. This will enable you to see which foods are not important to you and those you would not miss. Your extravagance could be the peanuts in the dish, an open box of chocolates or the remains of a packet of biscuits.

How and when you start to diet is of less importance than the complete necessity of keeping to the diet. Note down the calorific values of everything you eat and consciously try to register daily whether or not you have eaten at home or out. If you are dining away from home several times a week, you will have to choose all low-calorie dishes, but you may relax and eat everything if these occasions are rare. Never say to yourself, 'I'm going out tonight so I may as well eat what I like all day.' Calories must be counted at all times. Gimmicky diets are always popular and are not harmful if followed for a short time, but prolonged slimming régimes must be nutritionally balanced. It is for this reason that I believe in calorie counting. Try and use the allowance wisely, including high-protein foods, as well as a little fat to oil the works, in addition to salad items.

Carbohydrates include both starches and sugars and it is the sugars that contain what the nutritionists call 'empty calories'. In other words you are putting on weight without obtaining useful nutriment. There will, of course, be some foods which you dislike or that disagree with you. Many people are allergic to milk, and butter does not suit everyone. Cheese in its many forms can be substituted, provided the calories in total are of similar value. There is no advantage in cutting down on fluids unless they contain extra calories. Water costs nothing. But you must include in your day's calorie allowance any drinks containing milk or sugar.

A balanced diet should include carbohydrates, proteins, fats, mineral salts, vitamins and water. Carbohydrates include sugar, starch and cellulose. Sugar is not only what is added to sweeten foods, but also the natural sugar found in fruits. Starch is found in pasta, potatoes, bread and cereals. Cellulose is the indigestible part of fibrous vegetables. These vegetables and the bran in wholemeal bread are good for roughage, which helps in body-waste elimination. The sugar in milk is important although not essential.

Bread and cereals, although basically carbohydrates, also contain protein, Vitamin B and iron.

Protein is vital for bone building and renewal of the cells. It mainly comes from fish, meat, milk, eggs, cheese and nuts. Although 175 g (6 oz) of any one of these foods should be enough for one day's supply of protein, it is better to have a mix of protein intake.

Fats are not really necessary in a slimmer's diet, but a little butter or margarine is important, because these contain Vitamins A and D. Vitamin A is in fish livers, meat liver, egg yolks and dairy products. As carotene, it is contained in all red, orange and dark green vegetables. Of the B Vitamins, Thiamine B1 combats loss of appetite, indigestion and nervous irritability. Strangely enough, it is the vitamin that alcoholics are deficient in. Riboflavine B2 combats anaemia, sore lips and other inflammation. Niacin helps the proteins, carbohydrates and fats to function properly, and a regular intake of this vitamin maintains a healthy skin. Niacin is contained in meat, whole grain cereals, nuts, liver and yeast. Vitamin C is in all citrus fruits, and there is a day's allowance in one orange, or half a grapefruit, or one glass of fruit juice. Vitamin C is good for the skin and is supposed to stave off colds, provided it is taken in large enough doses. Vitamin D is the sunshine vitamin and, because we don't all get enough of it, our food may be fortified, as in margarine. It is also contained in egg yolks, liver, fatty fish and milk.

Iron is the best known mineral salt and is in offal, eggs, sardines, flour and even cocoa. The remaining mineral salts, iodine calcium, sodium, potassium and a few others are distributed throughout the normal diet.

Provided you have a little of everything, you should not have to worry about the proper balance of your food, as in a normal low-calorie diet this is quite adequately preserved.

Ready prepared basic ingredients are a boon to slimmers, since many people find it pointless to spend ages cooking a diet meal, particularly if it is for one only. Frozen vegetables, fish and chicken portions can be bought in bulk for freezer storage, enabling the hungry eater to restrict herself to the exact quantity required. Apart from freezer items, convenience foods may be canned or dehydrated. Ready-to-cook soups, main courses and desserts eliminate all the preparation, and boil-in-the-bag meals have the advantage of saving washing-up.

Canned foods are now available in different sizes, among which are a good selection of single servings. Always buy the size needed for one particular meal and then you will not be tempted to finish the rest. Remember Bing Crosby was the only person ever able to eat just half a biscuit. One of his lesser-known talents!

Ready-to-cook-and-serve dishes often have the calorie content printed on the package – these do not necessarily have to be specialized diet meals. This type of convenience food is invaluable, provided the calories are stated, but you must avoid any that require additional fat or sugar. This applies particularly to foods requiring frying. Ready-to-fry crumbed foods, such as stuffed pancakes, fish cakes and fish fingers, can be just as tasty when grilled or baked. You may find it helpful to use a non-stick baking sheet or to line an ordinary baking sheet with non-stick paper. It is well worth the small trouble.

Major manufacturers produce wide ranges of ready-to-cook dishes, including such delicacies as Prawn Curry (110 calories), Chicken Suprème and vegetables or Chilli Con Carne at under 250 calories. Among the canned selections are Sliced Roast Beef in Gravy (140 calories) and Shepherds Pie at a mere 238 calories. Low-calorie canned soups come to about 50 calories for a really full plate. Not all such foods are specifically prepared for the slimmer and manufacturers are increasingly printing calorie ratings on all their goods, so it would be worth having a closer look at those you have avoided in the past.

A SAMPLE 1000 CALORIE DIET

Daily Allowance of:	*Calories*
300 ml (½ pint) skimmed milk for tea and coffee	100
15 g (½ oz) low-calorie spread	50

Breakfast

1 rasher back bacon, well grilled	60
1 small boiled egg	70

Lunch

100 g (4 oz) grilled rump steak	200
large salad	50
1 orange	40

Evening meal

175 g (6 oz) grilled lemon sole	150
175 g (6 oz) jacket potato	150
2 tablespoons green peas	30
150 ml (¼ pint) made-up jelly	95

Total: *995 calories*

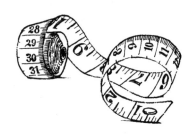

A SAMPLE 1500 CALORIE DIET

Daily Allowance of:	*Calories*
300 ml (½ pint) skimmed milk	100
25 g (1 oz) low-calorie spread	105

Breakfast

25 g (1 oz) cornflakes	100
1 small boiled egg	70
1 thin slice of toast	70
120 ml (4 fl. oz) grapefruit juice	40

Lunch

3 grilled chipolatas	240
100 g (4 oz) mashed potatoes	100
2 tablespoons sweetcorn	40
small banana	65

Evening Meal

50 g (2 oz) prawns	60
2 teaspoons low-calorie salad dressing	25
lettuce	—
100 g (4 oz) lean lamb chump chop, grilled	185
1 tomato, halved and grilled	10
175 g (6 oz) boiled cauliflower	30
1 small 142 ml carton fruit yogurt	150

Extras

25 g (1 oz) Camembert	90
1 crispbread	25

Total: *1500 calories*

NUTRITIONAL CHART

Some nutrients should be taken daily but, if you aim to balance out your intake over an average week, this will normally be acceptable. It is important to take enough protein in a diet; men require a minimum of 40 to 45 g protein daily and women 35 to 40 g. Since this book is aimed at those who entertain, only recommendations for adults are given. The fat and carbohydrate intakes are of less importance.

The figures in the following chart have been extracted from information given by the Ministry of Agriculture, Fisheries and Food.

Food per oz	Protein grams	Fat grams	Carbo-hydrate grams	Iron milligrams	Vitamins
almonds	5·8	15·2	1·2	1·2	B
apples	0·1	0	3·4	0·1	A, B, C
bacon	3·1	13·6	0	0·3	B
bananas	0·3	0	5·5	0·1	A, B, C
barley	2·2	0·5	23·7	0·2	B
beans, canned	1·7	0·1	4·9	0·6	A, B, C
beans, runner	0·3	0	0·8	0·2	A, B, C
beef	4·2	8·0	0	1·1	B
bread, starch reduced	3·0	0·4	13·5	0·4	B
bread, white	2·4	0·5	15·5	0·5	B
bread, wholemeal	2·7	0·9	13·2	0·9	B
Brussels sprouts, raw	1·0	0	1·3	0·2	A, B, C
Brussels sprouts, cooked	0·7	0	0·5	0·2	A, B, C
butter	0·1	23·4	0	0	A, D
cabbage, boiled	0·2	0	0·4	0·1	A, B, C
carrots	0·2	0	1·5	0·2	A, B, C
cheese, Cheddar	7·2	9·8	0	0·2	A, B, D
cheese, cottage	4·3	1·1	1·3	0·1	A, B, D

Food per oz	Protein grams	Fat grams	Carbo-hydrate grams	Iron milligrams	Vitamins
chicken	5·9	1·9	0	0·4	B
chocolate, drinking	1·6	1·9	25	3·4	B, C
coffee	0	0	0	0	B
cornflakes	2·1	0·1	24·9	0·3	B
eggs	3·4	3·5	0	0·7	A, B, D
fish fillets, white	4·5	0·1	0	0·3	B
fish fingers	3·8	1·9	5·9	0·4	B
flour	2·8	0·3	22·7	0·5	B
ham	4·6	11·2	0	0·7	B
herring	4·5	4	0	0·4	A, B, D
kidney	4·8	1·2	0	3·8	A, B, C
kipper	5·4	4·5	0	0·6	A, B, D
lamb	3·7	8·8	0	0·6	B
lemons	0·1	0	0·5	0	B, C
liver	4·7	2·3	0	3·9	A, B, C, D
margarine	0·1	24·3	0	0·1	A, D
milk, liquid, whole	0·9	1·1	1·4	negligible	A, B, C, D
milk, skimmed, liquid	1·1	0·1	1·3	negligible	A, B, C
oatmeal	3·4	2·5	20·6	1·2	B
oils	0	28·3	0	0	A, D
oranges	0·2	0	2·4	0·1	A, B, C
peaches, canned	0·1	0	6·5	0·5	A, B, C
peas, canned	2·0	0	5·1	0·3	A, B, C
pork	3·4	11·4	0	0·3	B
potatoes, boiled	0·4	0	5·6	0·1	B, C
rhubarb	0·2	0	0·3	0·1	A, B, C
rice	1·8	0·3	0·3	0·1	B
salmon, canned	5·6	1·7	0	0·4	A, B, D
spaghetti	2·8	0·3	23·8	0·3	B
spinach	0·8	0	0·8	0·9	A, B, C
strawberries	0·3	0	1·8	0·2	A, B, C
tea	0	0	0	0	B
tomatoes	0·3	0	0·8	0·1	A, B, C
yogurt, natural	1·0	0·7	1·5	0	A, B, D
yogurt, low-fat	1·0	0·1	1·5	0	A, B, D

WINES

Although almost 90 per cent water, wine also contains many valuable elements, making it a real liquid food. The calorific content depends on two factors: alcoholic strength and sugar content. The number of calories in a litre of wine varies between 600 and 1000. The lower level is for dry, white wines, and the number increases through red wines (700 to 800), to the Sauterne-type, sweet, soft white wines and, highest of all, dessert wines. Wine contains Vitamins C, C2, B2 and B3 and various mineral salts, and is an undoubted aid to digestion taken in reasonable amounts.

Wines make an excellent aperitif, preparing the organs for digestion by stimulating the secretion of gastric juices. Wine also contains enzymes similar to those present in the digestive juices, so, if you are tired, an aperitif can replace the natural function of the stomach to a certain extent. But there are aperitifs and aperitifs as far as the slimmer is concerned, and it is better to choose the wine-based drinks that don't need added spirits. Dry Martini is less high in calories than sweet Martini and, if you leave out the gin, the difference between a dry Vermouth (35 calories) and a gin and Dubonnet topped up with bitter lemon is 100 calories. Keep yourself to a measure of about 1 fl. oz, even if you give your guests generous quantities to help get the party going. Filling your glass with lots of ice also makes the drink go much further, and makes it look quite enormous.

Whether you serve red or white with your meal must depend on the main dish. Although there is a lot of chi-chi talk about what wine should go with what food, you must take some care if you are serving a particularly spicy or strongly flavoured recipe. To serve a delicate Alsace white with a full-bodied curry would kill the wine; and to serve a full-bodied red Burgundy would have the same effect, for example, on my recipe for Orange Buttered Plaice. Try, however, to keep to a dry white wine, which should be well chilled for a few hours before your guests arrive – there is no reason why you should not always keep a bottle in the refrigerator door against a sudden need. Never plunge a bottle into the freezer at the last moment. Better to find a bucket and gather as much ice as you can in the bucket around the bottle. I keep an emergency supply of ice cubes in the freezer in a plastic bag – they are very easy to separate by running hot water over the outside of the bag for a few seconds. White wine can be opened literally minutes before serving, but red wine is invariably better for de-corking – and better still decanting – an hour or so before the meal. The cheapest plonk can taste quite acceptable if it is poured from the bottle into a carafe, and there is no tell-tale label to give the game away.

The size of glass is fairly important. It is usual for white wine to be served in smaller goblets than red, but I believe you drink more from a small glass, repeatedly filled, than a larger glass filled once only. A 6 oz goblet is probably about right for white wines, but you need an 8 oz goblet for red wines, otherwise you don't get their full aroma.

Wines can be drunk several days after the bottle is opened. On the other hand, left-over wine is useful for cooking. You can even freeze it in cubes for future use. I deplore the way bottles of sherry and port are opened and only the odd drink served from them over months. By the time you get to the end of the bottle, there is no life or proper flavour left to the wine at all – it is discoloured and horribly sedimented.

Cooking with wine obviously adds calories to a dish. A quarter of a pint of dry white wine might add about 100 calories. As there is calorific value in both the alcohol and the sugar content, open-pan and flambé-style cooking – which causes the alcohol to evaporate – may lose 90 per cent of the original calorific value of the wine, while closed-pan cooking keeps most of the calories in the dish.

Finally a few words on liqueurs. These are useful, as they keep virtually for ever, so you can build up a choice over the years without fear of their going off. If you frequently travel abroad, you can afford to bring back unusual or undiscovered liqueurs at reasonable prices. However, drink for drink, liqueurs are high in calories and the slimmer should avoid them and, more particularly, port, which zooms up the calorific scale out of all proportion to the pleasures of its taste and digestive qualities.

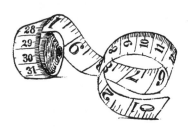

SLIMMERS' DREAM WEIGHT CHART

This weight chart is a realistic indication of what your weight should be. If you are more than 10 per cent in excess of this you would be considered a bad risk by an insurance company.

When studying the charts you must be realistic. Do not pick out the weight you think you should be, for you may never reach that goal. A practising sociable slimmer is unlikely to be pencil slim. She could only attain that by strictly disciplined dieting. Slim down as much as you can, but don't aim initially to reach the chart recommendations in one attack. When you have only 5 lbs surplus weight, you can reconsider and attempt the last few pounds if your will-power is sufficiently strong.

Weight is taken in the mornings before breakfast and without shoes or clothing. It is only necessary to weigh yourself once a week.

Females

Height		Small frame			Medium frame			Large frame		
ft	ins	kg*	st.	lbs	kg	st.	lbs	kg	st.	lbs
4	10	45	7	1	47	7	6	$50\frac{1}{2}$	7	13
4	11	46	7	3	$48\frac{1}{2}$	7	9	52	8	2
5	0	47	7	5	50	7	12	53	8	5
5	1	$48\frac{1}{2}$	7	9	$51\frac{1}{2}$	8	1	$54\frac{1}{2}$	8	8
5	2	50	7	12	53	8	5	56	8	11
5	3	51	8	0	54	8	7	57	9	0
5	4	52	8	3	56	8	10	59	9	4
5	5	53	8	5	57	8	13	61	9	8
5	6	56	8	10	60	9	6	$62\frac{1}{2}$	9	12
5	7	57	8	13	$60\frac{1}{2}$	9	7	64	10	1
5	8	58	9	2	62	9	10	66	10	5
5	9	60	9	6	$63\frac{1}{2}$	10	0	67	10	8
5	10	$61\frac{1}{2}$	9	9	65	10	3	$69\frac{1}{2}$	10	13
5	11	63	9	13	67	10	8	$71\frac{1}{2}$	11	3
6	0	66	10	5	69	10	12	72	11	5

* kilogram weights are to the nearest $\frac{1}{2}$ kg.

Males

Height		Small frame			Medium frame			Large frame		
ft	ins	kg*	st.	lbs	kg	st.	lbs	kg	st.	lbs
5	0	51	8	1	54	8	7	$58\frac{1}{2}$	9	3
5	1	52	8	2	55	8	9	$59\frac{1}{2}$	9	5
5	2	53	8	5	57	8	13	61	9	8
5	3	$54\frac{1}{2}$	8	8	58	9	2	$62\frac{1}{2}$	9	12
5	4	56	8	11	$59\frac{1}{2}$	9	5	64	10	1
5	5	57	9	0	61	9	8	66	10	5
5	6	$59\frac{1}{2}$	9	5	63	9	13	$67\frac{1}{2}$	10	9
5	7	61	9	8	65	10	3	70	11	0
5	8	63	9	13	$66\frac{1}{2}$	10	7	72	11	5
5	9	65	10	3	$68\frac{1}{2}$	10	11	74	11	9
5	10	$66\frac{1}{2}$	10	7	71	11	2	76	11	13
5	11	$68\frac{1}{2}$	10	11	$72\frac{1}{2}$	11	6	$79\frac{1}{2}$	12	7
6	0	$70\frac{1}{2}$	11	1	$74\frac{1}{2}$	11	10	$80\frac{1}{2}$	12	9
6	1	72	11	5	$76\frac{1}{2}$	12	1	$82\frac{1}{2}$	13	0
6	2	74	11	9	79	12	6	85	13	5
6	3	81	12	11	$81\frac{1}{2}$	12	12	$86\frac{1}{2}$	13	9

* kilogram weights are to the nearest $\frac{1}{2}$ kg

Calorie Guide for Basic Foods

Vegetables – per oz
(fresh and frozen have the same value)

	Calories		
aubergine	5	courgettes	negligible
bean sprouts	10	cucumber	negligible
beans, baked in tomato		leeks	10
sauce	25	marrow	negligible
broad	10	mushrooms	negligible
butter	25	onions	5
French	negligible	parsnips	15
kidney	25	peas	20
runner	5	peppers	5
beetroot	15	potatoes	25
broccoli	5	spinach	5
Brussels sprouts	5	spring greens	negligible
cabbage	5	swedes	5
carrots	5	sweet corn	30
cauliflower	5	tomatoes	5
celery	negligible	turnips	5

Fruits – per oz

Fresh

apples	10	grapefruit	5
apricots	10	grapes	15
bananas	20	lemons	negligible
blackberries	10	melon	10
blackcurrants	10	peaches	10
cherries	10	pears	10
gooseberries	10	pineapple	15

| plums | 10 | strawberries | 5 |
| raspberries | 5 | water melon | 5 |

Fruits – per oz

Dried

apricots	10	dates	60
cherries, glacé	60	figs	60
coconut, dessicated	180	prunes	40
currants	70	raisins	70
		sultanas	70

Fish – per oz

cockles	15	oysters	neglible
cod	20	plaice	20
coley	25	prawns	30
crab	35	salmon	50
haddock, fresh	20	scallops	20
haddock, smoked	30	scampi	30
hake	20	shrimps	30
halibut	40	skate	30
herring	65	sole	20
kipper	35	trout	30
mussels	25	winkles	25

Meat and poultry – per oz

bacon	90	pork	35
beef	50	rabbit	50
chicken	30	sausage, beef	60
duck	40	sausage, pork	100
kidney	35	tongue	70
lamb	95	turkey	30
liver	40	veal	30

Dairy produce – per oz

	Calories		
butter	225	Camembert	90
cheeses:		Cheddar	120
blue Stilton	120	Cheshire	110
Brie	90	cottage cheese	35

curd cheese	40	medium	80
cream cheese	130	large	90
Danish blue	105	white	15–20
Edam	90	milk per pint	
Gruyère	130	gold top	490
Leicester	105	red top	370
Parmesan	120	silver top	370
cream, double	130	skimmed	200
cream, single	60	evaporated, per fl. oz	45
cream, soured	55	condensed, sweetened,	
cream, whipping	105	per fl. oz	100
eggs, whole		condensed, unsweetened	
small	70	per fl. oz	45
		low-fat, powdered	20

Miscellaneous – per oz

	Calories		
		muesli	105
All Bran	90	pearl barley	100
arrowroot	100	porridge	115
Bread	70	rice	100
cornflakes	105	sago	100
cornflour	100	Shredded Wheat	105
custard powder	100	spaghetti	105
dripping	260	suet	260
flour	100	sugar	110
lard	260	vegetable oils	250
lentils	85	Weetabix	100
margarine	225	yogurt	from 15

Drinks

	Calories		Calories
Advocaat (1 fl. oz)	70	Cherry Brandy (1 fl. oz)	80
Alexandra (Brandy, Crème		Cider, dry ($\frac{1}{2}$ pint)	100
de Cacao and whipped		Cider, sweet ($\frac{1}{2}$ pint)	120
cream)	265	Cinzano Bianco	50
Babycham	60	Cinzano Rosso	45
Bitter ($\frac{1}{2}$ pint)	90	Coca Cola (6 fl. oz)	80
Bitter Lemon	40	Cointreau (1 fl. oz)	100
Bloody Mary	120	Dry Martini	35
Brandy (single measure)	65	Dubonnet	75
Campari Soda	70	Gin (single measure)	65

Gin and French	100	Sherry, dry (small schooner)	55
Gin and It	115	Sherry, sweet (small	
Gin and Tonic	95	schooner)	65
Ginger Ale	Nil	Snowball	80
Grapefruit Juice	70	Soda Water	Nil
Guinness (½ pint)	100	Sweet Martini	50
Lager (½ pint)	75	Tia Maria (1 fl. oz)	90
Lemonade	30	Tomato Juice (4 fl. oz)	30
Light Ale (½ pint)	90	Tonic Water	30
Lime Juice (1 fl. oz and		Vermouth (1 fl. oz)	45
water)	6	Vodka (single measure)	90
Mild (½ pint)	70	Whisky (single measure)	65
Orange Squash	40	Whisky and Ginger Ale	65
Pernod (1 fl. oz)	80	Whisky and Soda	65
Port (4 fl. oz)	185	White Lady	80
Rum (single measure)	65	Wine, red (4 fl. oz)	80
Rum and Coke	105	Wine, rosé (4 fl. oz)	75
Rum and Orange	105	Wine, white (4 fl. oz)	70

The measure, where not specifically noted, is for a usual-sized drink.

Index